METRE, RHYTHM AND VERSE FORM

Nobody can write about poetry without some idea of how it works, especially how it differs from prose. The principal distinction between prose and poetry is rhythm. This volume demonstrates the way in which rhythm interrelates with metre. It analyses the effects of rhythm in action and describes the forms of metre through which it manifests itself.

Metre, Rhythm and Verse Form is an invaluable introduction to the study of poetry. Philip Hobsbaum defines the difference between metre and rhythm, and provides new and precise definitions for such terms as blank verse, sprung verse and free verse. From the iambic foot to syllabics, and from the Shakespearean sonnet to the stepped verse of Sylvia Plath, this comprehensive and concise volume explains the terms and ideas which a student of literature is likely to encounter. It is a lucid guide through terminology and criticism which students will find essential reading.

Philip Hobsbaum is Professor of English Literature at Glasgow University. He is a poet and critic, and has chaired several influential writers' groups. His many publications include the Routledge English Text edition of *Wordsworth: Selected Poetry and Prose*.

D0778362

THE NEW CRITICAL IDIOM

SERIES EDITOR: JOHN DRAKAKIS, UNIVERSITY OF STIRLING

The New Critical Idiom is an invaluable series of introductory guides to today's critical terminology. Each book:

- provides a handy, explanatory guide to the use (and abuse) of the term
- offers an original and distinctive overview by a leading literary and cultural critic
- relates the term to the larger field of cultural representation.

With a strong emphasis on clarity, lively debate and the widest possible breadth of examples, *The New Critical Idiom* is an indispensable approach to key topics in literary studies.

- See below for new books in this series.

Gothic by Fred Botting
Historicism by Paul Hamilton
Ideology by David Hawkes
Metre, Rhythm and Verse by Philip Hobsbaum
Romanticism by Aidan Day

METRE, RHYTHM AND VERSE FORM

Philip Hobsbaum

LONDON AND NEW YORK

First published 1996
by Routledge
11 New Fetter Lane, London EC4P 4EE

Simultaneously published in the USA and Canada
by Routledge
29 West 35th Street, New York, NY 10001

Typeset in Adobe Garamond and Scala Sans
by Keystroke, Jacaranda Lodge, Wolverhampton

Printed and bound in Great Britain by
Clays Ltd, St Ives PLC

British Library Cataloguing in Publication Data
A catalogue record for this book is available from the British Library

Library of Congress Cataloguing in Publication Data
A catalogue record for this book has been requested

ISBN 0–415–12267–8 (hbk)
ISBN 0–415–08797–X (pbk)

For Paddy Lyons and John Christie

CONTENTS

SERIES EDITOR'S PREFACE

The New Critical Idiom is a series of introductory books which seeks to extend the lexicon of literary terms, in order to address the radical changes which have taken place in the study of literature during the last decades of the twentieth century. The aim is to provide clear, well-illustrated accounts of the full range of terminology currently in use, and to evolve histories of its changing usage.

The current state of the discipline of literary studies is one where there is considerable debate concerning basic questions of terminology. This involves, among other things, the boundaries which distinguish the literary from the non-literary; the position of literature within the larger sphere of culture; the relationship between literatures of different cultures; and questions concerning the relation of literary to other cultural forms within the context of interdisciplinary studies.

It is clear that the field of literary criticism and theory is a dynamic and heterogenous one. The present need is for individual volumes on terms which combine clarity of exposition with an adventurousness of perspective and a breadth of application. Each volume will contain as part of its apparatus some indication of the direction in which the definition of particular terms is likely to move, as well as expanding the disciplinary boundaries within which some of these terms have been traditionally contained. This will involve some re-situation of terms within the larger field of cultural representation, and will introduce examples from the area of film and the modern media in addition to examples from a variety of literary texts.

PREFACE

This book is designed to explain the most important component of verse; that is to say, its sound. Many poets hear the work they are about to compose before they know the words of their composition. The key component of sound is rhythm. Often it is the rhythm that decides the patterning of the words in a poem.

The terminology in which we speak of rhythm derives from the study of metre. Metre is the ground-plan or blueprint of a rhythmic structure. It may give us a basic sense of shape but it is the beginning of discussion rather than its process. It is rhythm that gives life to metre. We perceive the rhythm best by reading the poem aloud.

Of course it is possible to appreciate poetry without knowing how it is made. The appreciation, however, may be enhanced by an awareness of how poets work. Much more may be heard in a poem if one is consciously aware of its rhythmic structure.

The author of this book, hereinafter designated 'the present author', has had four collections of poems published. He was also trained as an actor. Some such practical experience as this is as necessary as the discipline of the scholar in writing about prosody, which has been called the grammar of poetry.

The present author would like to acknowledge the predecessor in this line of study to whom he owes much: the late G. S. Fraser, who was himself a poet as well as a critic. Help from Paul Fletcher, of the Glasgow University Library, in compiling a bibliography was of inestimable use. From the material gathered, the bibliography published at the end of this book is only the most exiguous selection. Further, without two terms' study leave granted by the University of Glasgow, the work would have been much longer in the undertaking.

Mrs Pat Devlin of Glasgow University helped considerably the secretarial side of this work. Dr Rex Mitchell, of the Queen's University of Belfast, gave valuable and patient instruction in the use of the computer on which the final draft was written, and Desmond O'Brien and Jean Anderson came to the rescue at dangerous corners. The present author gladly acknowledges dialogue with Rosemary, his wife; with the poet, Peter Redgrove; and with Dr John Drakakis, general editor of The New Critical Idiom series, who commissioned this book. Discussion with the English Literature staff seminar in the Institute of English Studies at the University of Warsaw proved useful. Especial thanks are owed to Dr Krzysztof Mościcki and to the late Professor Wanda Rulewicz; and to Professor Emma Harris OBE, Director, for inviting me to her distinguished institute in the first place.

The ears of the present author have been opened to several aspects of the subject by working with the actor John Christie and with the scholar Paddy Lyons. To these two friends the book is dedicated.

ACKNOWLEDGEMENTS

The publishers would like to express their thanks to the copyright holders for permission to reprint from the following:

'Still-Life' by Elizabeth Daryush, *Selected Poems*, 1985, Carcanet Press Limited; 'To a Snail' by Marianne Moore, *The Complete Poems of Marianne Moore*, 1984, Faber & Faber Ltd; 'Considering the Snail' by Thom Gunn, *My Sad Captains*, 1993, Faber & Faber Ltd; 'Revenge Fable' by Ted Hughes, *Crow: From the Life and Songs of the Crow*, 1972, Faber & Faber Ltd; 'The Snow Man' by Wallace Stevens, *Collected Poems*, 1955, Faber & Faber Ltd ; 'The Widow's Lament in Springtime' by William Carlos Williams, *Collected Poems*, 1994, Carcanet Press Limited; 'Ghosts' by Peter Redgrove, *The Moon Disposes*, 1987, Secker and Warburg; 'My Cats' by Stevie Smith, *The Collected Poems of Stevie Smith.* Copyright © 1972 by Stevie Smith. Reprinted by permission of New Directions Publishing Group and Penguin 20th Century Classics/James MacGibbon; 'In the village pond . . . ' by James Kirkup, *Shooting Stars*, 1992, Hub Editions; 'In a Station of the Metro' by Ezra Pound, *Collected Shorter Poems*, 1968, Faber & Faber Ltd; 'Siesta of a Hungarian Snake' by Edwin Morgan, *Collected Poems*, 1990, Carcanet Press Limited; 'Paid on both sides' by W.H. Auden, *Collected Poems*, 1976, ed. Edward Mendelson, Faber & Faber Ltd; 'Gerontion', 'The Waste Land' and 'Little Gidding' by T.S. Eliot, *Collected Poems 1909–1962*, 1974, Faber & Faber Ltd; 'Crossings xxxvi' by Seamus Heaney, *Seeing Things*, 1991, Faber & Faber Ltd; 'Station Island' by Seamus Heaney, *Station Island*, 1984, Faber & Faber Ltd; 'Lady Lazarus' by Sylvia Plath, *Ariel*, 1968, Faber & Faber Ltd; 'Sonnet: To Eva' by Sylvia Plath, *Collected Poems*, edited with an introduction by Ted Hughes, 1981, Faber & Faber Ltd.

Every effort has been made to contact the copyright holders concerned. Where credit has not been properly given, we would invite copyright holders to contact the publisher in the first instance.

1

METRE AND RHYTHM

English verse is a succession of syllables. Some are strongly emphasized, some are not. The pattern of metre is set up by the way in which heavily stressed syllables are interspersed with more lightly stressed syllables. The metrical patterns are termed 'feet'. The main types of feet are as follows.

The iamb: this consists of one lightly stressed syllable followed by one stressed syllable. 'Revolve', 'behind', 'before', 'aloud' are all iambs.

The trochee is the iamb reversed. It consists of one stressed and one lightly stressed foot. 'Forward', 'backward', 'rabbit', 'orange' are all trochees.

These two metrical feet, iamb and trochee, each consist of two syllables. But it is possible to have three syllables in a foot, as follows.

An anapaest consists of two lightly stressed syllables followed by one stressed syllable. 'Repossess' and 'understand' are examples.

A dactyl is an anapaest reversed. It consists of one stressed syllable followed by two lightly stressed syllables. 'Pulverize' and 'agitate' are dactylic feet.

The intermediate pattern, when a stressed syllable is flanked fore and aft by two lightly stressed syllables, is called an amphibrach: 'redouble', 'confetti'.

Such examples as are given here should not be taken to be fixed, as a mathematical quantity would be. They should be regarded rather as indicators. The weight of stress can vary appreciably according to context, especially when that context departs from a metrical norm.

What is a metrical norm? In order to form a line of verse, each foot is repeated several times. The more times the foot is repeated, the longer the line becomes.

It should be emphasized that one rarely comes across a line that is entirely anapaestic, or entirely dactylic, or entirely amphibrachic. Usually, with a line made up of trisyllabic feet, there is a mixture of patterns.

A dimeter is what we would call a line consisting of two feet. An iambic dimeter would be 'The passive heart'. A trochaic dimeter would be 'chimney sweeper'. One that is anapaestic is 'at the end of the road'. The equivalent dactyl would be 'Come along rapidly' and the equivalent amphibrach would be 'As midsummer flower'.

In practice this particular pattern tends to be mixed, as in the following start of an anonymous song of the sixteenth century:

> Over the mountains
> And under the waves,
> Over the fountains
> And under the graves.

The first and third lines are dactylic dimeters. The second and fourth lines, also dimeters, are amphibrachic, and docked of a final syllable.

The dimeter is rare, and the trimeter, in which three stressed syllables are in question, is scarcely less so. 'The world a hunting is' (William Drummond, 1585–1649) is an example of iambic trimeter. The trochaic equivalent is 'Rose-cheeked Laura, come' (Thomas Campion, 1567–1620), with the final syllable docked. An example of anapaestic trimeter is 'As we rush, as we rush, in the train' (James Thomson, 1834–82). A dactylic trimeter in a pristine state would be 'merrily, merrily, merrily', but the final syllable is usually docked.

Comparatively few poems of any worth have been written in very short lines. However, the American poet J. V. Cunningham (1911–85) was a master in this form of verse. Here is the poem from which an example of iambic dimeter, cited earlier, was culled. It is called 'Acknowledgment' and concerns the way in which an unimpressive life can be made meaningful in a literary text:

Your book affords
The peace of art,
Within whose boards
The passive heart

Impassive sleeps,
And like pressed flowers,
Though scentless, keeps
The scented hours.

More usually, short lines are variegated, in the manner of John Skelton (1460–1529). The mode is called 'Skeltonics', after him. His lyric 'To Mistress Margaret Hussey' begins:

Merry Margaret,
As midsummer flower,
Gentle as falcon
Or hawk of the tower.

The first foot of the first line is a docked dactyl, with a syllable elided from 'Merry'. We know this is docked, or truncated, because the mode of the poem is couched predominantly in feet of three syllables; that is to say, trisyllabic feet. Predominantly these feet are amphibrachic dimeters – 'As midsummer flower' – though there are also truncated dactylic dimeters – 'Gentle as falcon'.

Modern instances of Skeltonics have been produced by Robert Graves (1895–1985), who was a great admirer of the older poet, and by Lilian Bowes Lyon (1895–1949). She has them as dimeters in her poem 'Snow Bees'. This begins:

> Close friends we have
> Still in the womb,
> Or dumb in the grave.
> About us they come.

Trimeters displaying three sets of triple feet are used mainly for satirical purposes. There is little good poetry written in this pattern, but some that is entertaining. Winthrop Mackworth Praed (1802–39) uses an amphibrachic trimeter to celebrate the 'season'. This was a period of balls and parties held in London each year in the nineteenth and twentieth centuries, and discontinued only in recent times. It acted as a marriage mart for 'débutantes'; that is to say, young ladies thought socially acceptable enough to have been introduced to the reigning monarch. ('Gay' here has its original use of 'merry' or 'blithe'.)

> Good-night to the Season! 'tis over!
>   Gay dwellings no longer are gay;
> The courtier, the gambler, the lover,
>   Are scattered like swallows away.

Notice that the alternate lines are docked of a syllable.

However, the shorter line that is most frequently used is not the dimeter or the trimeter but the tetrameter. The tetrameter is a four-stress line, whose 'beat' is provided by the syllables that bear a heavy stress, as distinct from those that are lightly stressed.

The greatest variety is provided by the iambic tetrameter. This was the chosen mode of two major poets, Andrew Marvell (1621–78), who was best known for his prose in his own time, and

Jonathan Swift (1667–1745), who is best known for his prose in ours.

The range of which this metrical pattern is capable may be seen in the following examples, First, there is the beginning of Marvell's poem 'To his coy mistress':

> Had we but world enough, and time,
> This coyness, lady, were no crime.
> We would sit down and think which way
> To walk and pass our long love's day.

Then there is a poem on what seems to be a quite different topic, Swift's ironic elegy or verse obituary for himself, 'Verses on the Death of Dr Swift':

> The time is not remote, when I
> Must by the course of nature die:
> When I foresee my special friends,
> Will try to find their private ends.

Marvell's love poem rises to a metaphysical contemplation of death, still in this same metre:

> But at my back I always hear
> Time's winged chariot hurrying near:
> And yonder all before us lie
> Deserts of vast eternity.

The poem by Swift, though primarily satirical, has passages of meditation:

> Indifference clad in wisdom's guise
> All fortitude of mind supplies:
> For how can stony bowels melt,
> In those who never pity felt?

The trochaic tetrameter, on the other hand, is capable of no such variegation. Swift is probably the greatest master of this limited metre, and he uses it mainly to express indignation. In 'The Legion Club', he gives his view concerning the Irish Parliament of his day:

> Let them, when they once get in,
> Sell the nation for a pin;
> While they sit a-picking straws,
> Let them rave of making laws;
> While they never hold their tongue,
> Let them dabble in their dung.

As with those in the trimeter, the triple feet employed in the tetrameter are chiefly useful in the lighter kind of satire. Matthew Prior (1664–1721) has a poem called 'A Better Answer', addressed to his presumed mistress, in which he whimsically discredits the truth of another poem he has written, apparently to some other young lady:

> Dear Chloe, how blubbered is that pretty face,
>   Thy cheek all on fire, and thy hair all uncurled,
> Prithee quit this caprice and, as old Falstaff says,
>   Let us e'en talk a little like folks of this world.

Notice that the final foot in each line is, as in earlier examples of amphibrachic metre, docked of a syllable.

So far, the argument of this chapter has been couched in terms of metre. But metre is by no means the whole of prosody, as the study of the art of versification is called. In fact, many practising poets would question whether problems of metre have much to do with 'art'. They are primarily a matter of craft: the kind of dexterity that, as the master-metrist Seamus Heaney (b. 1939) says, wins competitions in the weekly magazines. One certainly needs craft in order to write a poem, but a good deal else is necessary. One needs that set of faculties which Seamus Heaney calls 'technique': 'the whole creative effort of the mind's and body's resources to bring the meaning of experience within the jurisdiction of form'. We can use this differentiation between craft and technique in seeking to indicate what, more than metre, goes to creating the movement of a poem.

Metre is a blueprint; rhythm is the inhabited building. Metre is a skeleton; rhythm is the functioning body. Metre is a map; rhythm is a land.

The forms I have described in metrical terms can hardly ever be found practised with the simplicity that those terms suggest. What, more than metre, does a poem have? It has variegation of verse movement. The poet may indeed begin with a metrical plan. But that plan is realized in terms of variations; variations on a metrical norm.

This can be seen even in the examples quoted so far. There are syllables docked from the ends of lines, as in Praed's 'Good-night to the Season', already glanced at, and Prior's 'A Better Answer'. There are role-reversals, as when dactyls – 'Gentle as' – stand in for amphibrachs – 'Or hawk of'. But, more subtle than that, we have variegation of stress itself.

So far, we have been proceeding on the assumption that there are only two degrees of emphasis in syllables: stressed and lightly stressed. There are, in fact, four recognizable levels of emphasis: primary stress, secondary stress, tertiary stress and weak stress. Using a system developed in 1951 by the linguists George L. Trager and Henry Lee Smith, we can represent primary stress (heavy) with ´; secondary stress (medium) with ^; tertiary stress (medium-light) with `; and weak stress (light) with ˘.

This mode of representation may serve as a way of indicating the difference in rhythmic structure between verse patterns that seem metrically identical. The end of a foot may be represented with a bar, thus: |.

Earlier on, the iambic tetrameter was characterized as offering a greater range than the metres previously considered, the dimeter and the trimeter. Four beats are better than two or three, at least so far as variety is in question. If we take the two quotations from

Marvell's 'To His Coy Mistress', the point can be made by utilizing
the Trager–Smith notation:

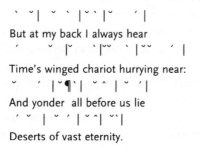

Had we but world enough, and time

This coyness, lady, were no crime.

We would sit down and think which way

To walk and pass our long love's day.

The first foot of the first line, when we come to look at it rhythmically rather than metrically, is inverted. That is to say, the
iambic norm would lead us to expect a light stress on the first
syllable, 'had', and a heavier stress on the second syllable, 'we'. The
reverse is true. Yet the stress in this first foot is not the heaviest you
can get. The main emphasis in the line is on 'world' and on 'time',
and appositely so, since these – rather than persuading one's
mistress to bed – are the main themes of the poem. Therefore these
two words take the heaviest stresses, the *primary* stresses.

The poem builds up its preoccupation with 'world' and 'time' to
this extent, that sixteen lines further on it has gravitated into a
sense of urgency regarding death. The metre is the same; the
rhythmic structure shows some interesting differences:

But at my back I always hear

Time's winged chariot hurrying near:

And yonder all before us lie

Deserts of vast eternity.

There is a greater sense of speed in this passage, compared with the previous one quoted. This is in part accomplished by there being a greater proportion of light stresses to those that are heavy, and more of those supposedly heavy stresses are secondary and tertiary than is the case with the previous example. The line 'Time's winged chariot hurrying near', in consequence, really does hurry: the rhythm acts out the sense.

In the next line, 'And yonder all before us lie', there is a noticeable pause between 'yonder' and 'all', and this has been marked with ¶. The effect is to allow a medium-light stress on 'all', so as not to slow the rhythm up too much. This kind of pause plays an important part in versification. In fact, there is almost always a pause mid-line called a caesura. Usually it is too slight to require a special marking. Further, the end of every line in every poem has a pause. Again, it is not usually marked as a separate item. However, it is this that, in the present instance, allows the weight of 'lie', with its heavy stress, to continue without merging into the next line. It is in this way that we can have a heavy stress on 'lie' and a heavy stress on the first syllable of 'Deserts' without destroying the basic metre. The effect is as though a silent but noticeable equivalent of ˘ had been interposed.

In this final line of the passage cited, the disposition of stresses allows the rhythm to trail off, as it were, *into* the deserts. After the first, each successive one of the so-called heavier stresses in this line of verse – 'Deserts of vast eternity' – is in effect lighter than the last. After the heavy stress on the first syllable of 'Deserts', there is a further heavy stress on 'vast', but then there is a medium stress on the second syllable of 'eternity', and a medium-light stress on the fourth syllable. This is in contradistinction to what happened in the first four lines quoted from 'To His Coy Mistress', where every line ended with a heavy stress, thus slowing the rhythm down. This contradistinction accounts for the difference in *rhythm* between the two quatrains, or groups of four lines, even though the *metre* is ostensibly the same.

2

BLANK VERSE

Blank verse is the most important metre in English. It is the metre in which most of the great poetry has been written.

It is unrhymed. It consists of five iambic feet in a line, notated thus:

˘ ´ | ˘ ´ | ˘ ´ | ˘ ´ | ˘ ´ |

The line usually occupies the time taken by a breath, and therefore is suitable for dramatic performance. It also has the advantage of considerable variety in rhythm, which allows it to represent a range of style quite unequalled by other metres.

Blank verse was first used in English by the Earl of Surrey (?1517–47). It is the metre chosen for his translation of the *Aeneid*, an epic originally written in Latin by Virgil (70–19 BC). An epic is a large-scale narrative poem on an exalted theme, usually concerned with crisis in a race or culture. Surrey used blank verse as an equivalent to the Latin heroic line, the hexameter, for which there is no exact equivalent in English.

In the hands of Surrey, blank verse is very much a pioneering medium. It is highly conscious of the need to establish a norm, and consequently is more formal in its expression than later attempts at the metre. In other words, the rhythm conforms very closely to its metrical blueprint. The following passage comes from the beginning of Book II in Surrey's translation:

> They whisted all, with fixëd face attent,
> When Prince Æneas from the royal seat
> Thus gan to speak: O Queen, it is thy will
> I should renew a woe cannot be told!
> How that the Greeks did spoil and overthrow
> The Phrygian wealth and wailful realm of Troy.

To write as metrically as this is to risk losing the attention of the reader. There are many more rhythmic possibilities than the extract just cited suggests. The versatility of blank verse permits the identification of many varieties within the metre. Three of these may be held to predominate. After the greatest poets with whom they are associated, they may be termed Miltonic blank verse, Shakespearian blank verse and Wordsworthian blank verse.

John Milton (1608–74) used blank verse as the medium of *Paradise Lost*, a poem describing the Fall of Man in the Garden of Eden. It is probably the poem in English nearest to the classical epic as represented by Virgil's *Aeneid*. Even so, it does not keep so closely to the metrical norm as Surrey's translation. Milton does not give us an expected pattern of five light stresses alternating with five heavy stresses. The norm of his rhythmic pattern is established at the beginning of *Paradise Lost*. But if we scan it using the Trager–Smith notation, the rhythm will be found significantly to vary its metrical basis:

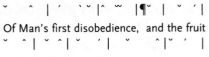

Of Man's first disobedience, and the fruit

Of that forbidden tree whose mortal taste

˄   ´ |¶ ˇ|ˇ ˇ   ´ | ˇ   ˄| ˇ ˇ   ´ |

Brought death into the World, and all our woe,

ˇ   ˄ |ˇ   ´|ˇ ¶| ˇ ˇ   ´ | ˇ   ´ |

With loss of Eden,   till one greater Man

ˇ   ´ | ˇ ¶| ˇ   ˇ   ˇ   ˄| ˇ   ˄| ˇ   ´ |

Restore us,   and regain the blissful seat,

´   ¶| ´   ˇ   ˇ| ´ |

Sing,   Heavenly Muse . . .

Because all stresses vary, and no two stresses need have exactly
the same value, the blank verse line cannot go:

ˇ ´|ˇ ´|ˇ ´|ˇ ´|ˇ ´|

In this particular example, some of the lighter stresses that in other
poets might be represented as ` here sound as ˄. That is to say, they
are medium rather than medium-light, because of the weight and
emphasis of the verse. The verse also has more by way of pause – ¶
– substituting for foot, because of the relative slowness of the
rhythm.

Take that first line:

Of Man's first disobedience, and the fruit . . .

The key stresses come on 'first' and 'fruit', a weight determined
not only by rhythm but by meaning. It is this *first* disobedience
of many that is in question, and this disobedience took place
through the defiance of God's law in eating the forbidden *fruit*.
But one cannot ignore the basic metre, any more than one can
ignore the identity of the sinner – Man – and so one has to put
the second most weighty kind of stress, medium rather than
medium-light, on 'Man's' and on the operative part of 'disob*edi*-
ence'. Since the two last syllables of 'disobedience' are the lightest
you can have, and since they are followed by two more light
syllables, 'and the', clearly there is some kind of pause between
these two groups:

˘˘ | ¶ ˘| ˘
-ience,   and the

Otherwise the metre would be lost and the rhythm would collapse. The pause here is the equivalent of a further medium stress. That is to say, in this instance, ¶ = ˆ.

So in rhythmic, as distinct from metrical, terms, the scansion of the first line of *Paradise Lost* is:

˘   ˆ | ´   ` ˘|ˆ ˘ |¶˘ | ˘   ´|
Of Man's first disobedience, and the fruit . . .

Of course, this scansion derives from a particular reading, and another way of reading the line is possible. There will always be a certain amount of choice in rhythmic scansion, since rhythm is a matter of hearing the verse rather than counting the syllables, and no two people are going to hear the verse in exactly the same way. What is required is not an adherence to rule but the discovery of a pattern that makes sense to oneself and to other readers. Given the subject-matter and the resonance of the verse of *Paradise Lost*, any reading that quickens the rhythm will trivialize the meaning. To omit the pause after 'disobedience' would be unduly to hurry the rhythm and could lead only to misunderstanding. These three factors – rhythm, the sound of the language, and the meaning of the language – are, in practice, inseparable. In practice, we hear the poem as a single entity. It is only for the purposes of analytical discussion such as this that its elements can be separated at all.

The way in which Milton uses rhythm is different from that of William Shakespeare (1564–1616), even though both the younger and the older poet wrote in blank verse. The range of Shakespeare is greater and his tone more flexible than that of Milton, as befits a writer essentially of dramatic poetry. He goes in much more than Milton for sudden contrasts of rhythm, amounting almost to a breaking-up of the line, a disjuncture. Shakespeare's syntax too – the grammatical relationships between his words – is considerably more free. Sometimes, if we consult the grammar books, it will be found to be outside conventional usage.

In the play *Macbeth*, the titular hero has enticed into his house and murdered Duncan, his benefactor, friend and kinsman – who is also his king. This is a crime which merits no forgiveness, yet Macbeth behaves as though he deserves mercy.

In Act I Scene VII of *Macbeth* we have this murderer who has the soul of a poet seeking to plan the death of the king at the same time as he ransacks his conscience in a kind of disastrous stock-taking. There is a metre discernible here, as there is in Milton, but one that is broken up, almost disrupted. It is as though, in taking leave of rational behaviour, Macbeth is in process of losing control of forms of expression:

> If it were done when 'tis done, then 'twere well
> It were done quickly: if th'assassination
> Could trammel up the consequence, and catch
> With his surcease success; that but this blow
> Might be the be-all and the end-all here,
> But here, upon this bank and shoal of time
> We'd jump the life to come.

The time is sick here, and the verse rhythm sways and slews with it. We recognize this as blank verse in the same way as we know that a Rottweiler and a fox-terrier are of the same species. Neither animal could be anything but a dog, and, in much the same way, this passage could be nothing but blank verse. The details of the metre may seem to vary, but there is a pattern pulsing through of five heavy or medium stresses to a line.

The first line has two tremendous stresses on 'done', like the tolling of a great bell, with medium stresses coming on 'if' and 'well'. The latter is stretched out on the rack of conjecture by its position as the last word in the line. It therefore latches on to that almost infinitesimal pause that acts as a silent punctuation at the end of each line of verse – that helps, in fact, to *make* it a line of verse.

There is one resemblance to Milton, though. Shakespeare often puts a stress on a caesura or pause in mid-line. Usually a caesura need not be marked. Here, it has to be. It can be presumed quite definitely at the end of this first phrase, after 'done':

˄ ˇ | ˇ   ´ | ˋ   ˇ   ´ | ¶ | ˇ   ˇ   ˄ |
If it were done when 'tis done,   then 'twere well . . .

It is possible to make the silence speak, as it does here, if the pregnant pause is surrounded with an appropriate patterning of heavy stress and medium stress interspersed with light stresses – the so-called weak syllables, 'it', 'were', 'when', ''tis', 'then', ''twere'.

That, however, is not enough to make Shakespeare sound like Milton, and the difference is to be expressed rhythmically rather than metrically. In Milton, there is a tendency towards the heavier stress, a use of pause that appreciably slows the rhythm down, a reliance on the more resonant vowel sounds, a vocabulary derived from the Latin and in other ways 'literary' – that is to say, departing from the representation of colloquial speech. All this is a description of rhythm rather than one of metre.

What is true of Shakespearian verse in contrast to Miltonic blank verse is true also of William Wordsworth (1770–1850) in contrast to Shakespeare. There are, rhythmically speaking, several Wordsworths as there are several Shakespeares. There is Wordsworth hortatory; being heard by the crowd, so to speak:

Wisdom and Spirit of the universe!
Thou Soul that art the eternity of thought.

There is Wordsworth, only a few lines further on in *The Prelude*, being narrative, telling a story:

And in the frosty season, when the sun
Was set, and visible for many a mile
The cottage windows through the twilight blazed.

Perhaps most individual of all, there is Wordsworth retrospective, remembering things past:

> This boy was taken from his mates, and died
> In childhood, ere he was full ten years old.
> – Fair are the woods, and beauteous is the spot,
> The vale where he was born; the churchyard hangs
> Upon a slope above the village school,
> And there, along that bank, when I have passed
> At evening, I believe that oftentimes
> A full half-hour together I have stood
> Mute, looking at the grave in which he lies.

Metrically, this is a derivation from Milton refracted through the verse of a number of eighteenth-century poets, mostly seeking to write in a realistic vein, many of them unread now.

But rhythmically it is unlike Milton, or Shakespeare either. It tends to avoid the heavier stresses. In terms of stress, almost everything is medium to light. The verse is quiet in sound. While it moves, it seems scarcely to be moving. It is like the picture of a cloud in motion rather than that cloud above us in the sky.

One is driven into describing this, as so often with poetry, in terms not so much of stress as of voice. It is a quiet voice, the quietest of all voices. The lucidity of syntax and absence of resonance make it seem to issue from just inside the reader's own skull:

```
ˇ     ^ | ˇ ` | ˇ   ^ |   ˇ `| ˇ   ^   |
And there, along that bank, when I have passed
ˇ  ´| ˇ ˇ   `| ˇ ^ |  ˇ `| ˇ  ^  |
At evening, I believe that oftentimes
ˇ ^ |  ˇ    ` |ˇ  ˇ ` |ˇ `| ˇ    ^  | >
A full half-hour together I have stood
  ´  ¶ | ` ˇ | ˇ   ˇ  ^ | ˇ  ` | ˇ ´ |
Mute,   looking at the grave in which he lies.
```

There is a displacement of stress. One finds a reliance upon enjambment, represented here as >. That is to say, the sense, and therefore the rhythm, runs over the line:

˘ ^ | ˘   ` |˘  ˘ ` | ˘ ` | ˘   ^ | >
A full half-hour together I have stood

 ´   ¶|
Mute . . .

This brings the verse near to an internal discourse, that which Wordsworth himself called 'the still sad music of humanity . . . felt in the blood, and felt along the heart'. It is so quiet as scarcely to seem blank verse at all. Nor is it; not, at least, in the Miltonic sense.

Wordsworth himself said that his verse could best be identified *as* verse by its language. By this, he seems to have meant the appropriateness of diction – the vocabulary used in his poetry – rather than any poeticism that was calculated to draw attention to itself. The language here is simple: 'boy', 'mates', 'fair', 'spot', 'vale', 'village', 'school', 'bank, 'grave'. Such words represent simple but crucial stations, that take one from the cradle to the inevitable end. Wordsworth's diction helps to make this lightly stressed metre function as rhythm because it puts experience in perspective. It is more evocative of the key places in life than most prose could comparably be.

The use of metrical form by Milton, Shakespeare and Wordsworth has been discussed in terms of their rhythmical differences. If blank verse can sound so different from one poet to another, it suggests that the term 'blank verse' is a convenient pointer rather than a useful description, at least so far as rhythm is concerned. We have to think in terms of tendencies rather than set categories. If that is so, then the names of Milton, Shakespeare and Wordsworth can be used to denominate the three major kinds of blank verse usable down to the present time.

Miltonic blank verse was evident through the nineteenth

century, though it is less apparent today. It tended to be used by poets when they were turning to prophecy or making some publicly philosophical statement. Here is Alfred, Lord Tennyson (1809–92), in his Victorian attempt at an epic, *Idylls of the King*:

> And slowly answered Arthur from the barge:
> The old order changeth, yielding place to new
> And God fulfils Himself in many ways,
> Lest one good custom should corrupt the world.

This can be called 'Miltonic' because of its propensity towards using the heavier stresses, its preference for the more resonant vowel sounds, and its reliance on a 'literary' vocabulary, removed from any representation of speech.

Shakespearian blank verse was used by many Victorian poets, when they were attempting poetic drama. The vocabulary employed is less varied than that of Shakespeare, and significantly not many of these poetic dramas were ever staged. Robert Browning (1812–89) was perhaps the best of the Victorian exemplars of the art, but his most effective drama proved to be in his monologues. Though not intended for the stage, these are more actable and certainly more speakable than any of the speeches in his dramas proper. For example, 'Fra Lippo Lippi' begins with a monk escaped from his cloister being confronted by the city guards:

> I am poor brother Lippo, by your leave!
> You need not clap your torches in my face.
> Zooks, what's to blame? you think you see a monk!
> What, 'tis past midnight, and you go the rounds,
> And here you catch me at the alley's end
> Where sportive ladies leave their doors ajar?

This blank verse can be called Shakespearian because of its variegation of stress, its tendency towards contrasts in speed, and its consequent propensity towards disjuncture – near-breakage – in rhythm.

Browning's version of Shakespearian blank verse had its imitators through the nineteenth and early twentieth centuries, and did much to reify English poetry in the mid-century. George MacBeth (1932–92), significantly a radio producer as well as a poet, made especially inventive use of both dramatic monologue and of the Shakespearian mode of blank verse in which it tends to be couched. His 'Report to the Director' – a report after inspecting an extermination depot – begins:

> I'd say their marble cubicles were a shade
> Too small for the taller men, but they all appeared
> To be standing at ease. O the usual postures – hands
> In their pockets, hands on their hips, hands on the wall,
> A few touched themselves. A few were saying prayers.

This is freer in metre than Browning, but it takes off from that poet's tendency to represent the intonations of speech. For all its exclamations and turnings-aside from the subject in hand, it still utilizes a recognizably five-stress line.

But it is the *Wordsworthian* mode that appears to have had the most satisfactory run. It is peculiarly associated with recollection and with meditation. The nineteenth century has some fine examples of the latter. This is the beginning of 'Thanatopsis', a contemplation of death, by William Cullen Bryant (1794–1878):

> To him who in the love of Nature holds
> Communion with her visible forms, she speaks
> A various language; for his gayer hours
> She has a voice of gladness, and a smile
> And eloquence of beauty.

This would be recognized as Wordsworthian blank verse because of its absence of disjunctive pauses and its preference for medium stress in preference to the heavier stresses. It is, also, notably quiet in tone; an effect brought about by more muted vowel sounds and a less spectacular vocabulary. These matters may not be questions of metre, but they certainly have a great deal to do with rhythm.

In the twentieth century, perhaps the greatest master at once of Wordsworthian blank verse and of meditation is Wallace Stevens (1879–1955). Like Bryant, he is an American. Stevens's most famous poem is 'Sunday Morning', a contemplation of a godless universe. It begins:

> Complacencies of the peignoir, and late
> Coffee and oranges in a sunny chair,
> And the green freedom of a cockatoo
> Upon a rug mingle to dissipate
> The holy hush of ancient sacrifice.

That there are differences between the twentieth-century poets and their great predecessors is not under dispute. But the verse is recognizably the same today, with its basic five-stress metre. It retains the capacity for rhythmic variegation without losing the sense of verse form. The present author wrote a poem, 'The Rock Pool', about an incident in his childhood, and the form of blank verse came to him quite naturally as a vehicle for retrospect and meditation:

> My life could have ended then, crouched over the pool,
> Wedged against Huntcliff. Absorbed in its own life,
> Its pimpled sea-fronds and the slimy rocks
> Spangled with barnacles, the pool lay
> Deceptively clear to the sky, its wraiths of weed,
> Its floating upturned dead snails, the limpets
> Solidly bossed to the rock – I tried to prise them
> Into a free float, but cut my fingers
> And winced. Deep in the clefts stiff with mussels
> I pried, and under the weed that carpeted
> The pool bottom recoiled from a starfish, waylaid
> A crab – there he glared, squeezed little face

Tucked under his shell. And never noticed till
A wave sploshed into my pool, stirring up sludge,
Swathing crab, starfish, limpets too, in fog,
That the tide had come up, to my ears soundlessly,
Warning me off to my world, away from the sea.

Many upheavals have occurred since the Earl of Surrey first
crafted this versatile metre, but blank verse has never lost its place
as the central medium for English poetry.

3

THE HEROIC COUPLET

The heroic couplet resembles a blank verse line, inasmuch as the basic metre runs:

˘ ´ ˘ ´ ˘ ´ ˘ ´ ˘ ´

The difference is that the heroic couplet rhymes in pairs.

The rhyme scheme is notated as a a b b c c d d. Each individual letter betokens a new rhyme. Any coincidence of letters betokens the same rhyme, as follows:

When I consider life, 'tis all a cheat;	a
Yet, fooled with hope, men favour the deceit;	a
Trust on, and think tomorrow will repay:	b
Tomorrow's falser than the former day;	b
Lies worse, and, while it says, we shall be blest	c
With some new joys, cuts off what we possessed.	c
Strange cozenage! None would live past years again	d
Yet all hope pleasure in what yet remain;	d
And, from the dregs of life, think to receive,	e
What the first sprightly running could not give.	e
I'm tired with waiting for this chemic gold,	f
Which fools us young, and beggars us when old.	f

This is from *Aurung-Zebe*, by John Dryden (1631–1700), and one may feel surprised to find that it is a play. It is, in fact, a heroic tragedy; one akin to classical epic, whose heroes strike self-consciously noble attitudes. Hence the name of the metre: heroic couplet.

The mode of sententious moralizing, of which this is a fine example, rose in the early seventeenth century and dominated English poetry, throughout that century and its successor. Especially between 1640 and 1750, or thereabouts, it was how one wrote a long poem, dramatic or not.

The form of the heroic couplet was invented by Geoffrey Chaucer (1340–1400), often, and for other reasons, termed 'the father of English poetry'. It thus antedates the invention of blank verse by some 150 years. Chaucer's first exercise in the metre seems to have been his *Legend of Good Women*, which is usually dated to the mid-1380s. This is how one of its Prologues (there are two different versions) begins:

A thousand times have I heard men tell
That there is joy in heaven and pain in hell,
And I accorde well that it is so;
Yet natheless, yet wot I well also
That there is none dwelling in this country
That either hath in heaven or hell y-be,
Ne may of hit none other wayes witten
But as he hath heard said or found it written.

('Natheless' is the same as 'nonetheless'; 'wot' is the same as 'understand', and so is 'witten'; 'hit' is 'it'.)

The difference between this and the preceding passage from Dryden is that Chaucer sounds certain vowels that would not have been sounded in Dryden's time, much less in our own. These vowels are here put into bold print. The main vowel to receive this treatment in Chaucer, here as elsewhere, is *e*: 'A thousand times have I heard men tell'. Without that kind of sounding, the line would not scan as part of a heroic couplet.

Yet there is no agreement as to how Chaucer used this sounded *e*. The vowel seems to have been sounded or not sounded, according to whether a line would or would not scan without it. The device seems similar to the added syllable we find in this same passage: 'That either hath in heaven or hell y-be'. There is no grammatical necessity for the 'y-' here. It is just that, without the added syllable, the line would not scan.

Soon after Surrey's translation of Virgil, blank verse became a persuasive rival to the heroic couplet. It moved into most forms of drama. Yet the heroic couplet held its own as a vehicle for meditative and satiric poetry and, until Milton's example took hold some half-century after his death, as a vehicle for narrative poetry also.

One of the stories that circulate about English poetry is that the couplet at one point was very rough and was civilized by Dryden and other great poets of the late seventeenth century. It would be truer to say that, just as blank verse has three major varieties, so the heroic couplet has two. One of them can be associated with Dryden's greatest successor in the satiric mode, Alexander Pope (1688–1744). The famous poet, beset by fans who wish him only to look at their own verse, begs his servant to keep away from his secluded study these frenzied admirers:

> Shut, shut the door, good John! fatigued, I said,
> Tie up the knocker, say I'm sick, I'm dead.
> The dog-star rages! nay 'tis past a doubt,
> All Bedlam, or Parnassus, is let out.
> Fire in each eye, and papers in each hand,
> They rave, recite and madden round the land.

That is the beginning of Pope's Epistle – that is to say, a formal letter – to his friend Dr Arbuthnot. The 'dog-star' is Sirius, part of the constellation Canis Major (larger dog), and associated with the heat of August when dogs and poets go mad. Bedlam was a well-known lunatic asylum of the day, which the poet equates with Parnassus, the cradle of the Muses, who inspired the arts. It is a technically brilliant piece of verse, as anyone who wishes to write heroic couplets will discover in undertaking that particular metrical form. There is almost as much variegation of rhythm as you would find in a piece of dramatic blank verse:

> ˆ ˆ | ˘ ´ | ˘ ´ | ˘ ´ | ˘ ˆ |
>
> Shut, shut the door, good John! fatigued, I said;
>
> ´ ˘ | ˘ ´ | ˘ ` | ˘ ´ | ˘ ´ |
>
> Tie up the knocker, say I'm sick, I'm dead.

It may not be as varied as *Macbeth*, but it is far from adhering to a metrical norm.

Even so, we cannot help but be conscious of the rhymes lining themselves up like a double row of soldiers. For all the comparative freedom of rhythm, each pair of lines tends to be a closed entity.

Now this is not owing to the tyranny Pope exerted over the heroic couplet. Nor is it part of some civilizing process. There were couplets more metrically based than this being written over a hundred years earlier. The following is from a book of poems called *Bosworth Field* by Sir John Beaumont (1583–1627). It is the beginning of an elegy on his son:

> Can I, who have for others oft compiled
> The songs of death, forget my sweetest child,
> Which like the flower crushed with a blast is dead,
> And ere full time, hangs down his smiling head.

Line 3 seems slightly less regular than the others. 'Flower', though, would have been pronounced as a single syllable. The lines are, that is to say, related to the metrical norm:

> ˆ ˘ | ˘ ´ | ´ ˘ | ˘ ´ | ˘ ´ |
>
> Which like the flower crushed with a blast is dead . . .

No doubt what is behind this is another poem, also lamenting the death of a son, by a poet Sir John Beaumont greatly admired; at least, he wrote 'a song of death' in his honour. The poet in question is Shakespeare's great contemporary Ben Jonson (1572–1637); the poem, 'On my first son':

> Farewell, thou child of my right hand, and joy;
> My sin was too much hope of thee, loved boy,
> Seven years thou wert lent to me, and I thee pay
> Exacted by thy fate, on the just day.
> O, could I lose all father, now. For why
> Will man lament the state he should envy?
> To have so soon 'scaped world's, and flesh's rage,
> And, if no other misery, yet age!
> Rest in soft peace, and, asked, say here doth lie
> Ben Jonson his best piece of poetry.
> For whose sake, henceforth, all his vows be such,
> As what he loves may never like too much.

This is a poem much of whose appeal lies in control; the way in which a powerful emotion is contained in a set of heroic couplets, and does not overflow the line.

But that is only one variety of this particular metre. The same poet could write, in narrative vein:

> It was the day, what time the powerful moon
> Makes the poor Bankside creature wet its shoon,
> In its own hall; when these (in worthy scorn
> Of those, that put out monies, on return
> From Venice, Paris, or some inland passage
> Of six times to, and fro, without embassage,
> Or him that backward went to Berwick, or which
> Did dance the famous Morris, unto Norwich)
> At Bread Street's Mermaid, having dined, and merry,
> Proposed to go to Holborn in a wherry.

This is an extract from Jonson's scabrous poem 'On the Famous Voyage'; the voyage in question being through the poet's guts. 'Shoon' is an archaic plural for shoes; 'embassage' is a commission or message; 'backward to Berwick' – some person, not identifiable, must have attempted the feat of walking backwards, presumably from London, to the Scottish Border town of Berwick; 'the famous Morris' – the comedian Will Kemp danced from London to Norwich in 1599; 'wherry' – rowing-boat, designed to carry passengers on the river.

Two characteristics distinguish these heroic couplets from the ones used in Jonson's poem on his son, and indeed those used by Dryden, Pope and Beaumont. One is the extent to which the verse employs enjambment; that is to say, the extent to which the lines overflow their metrical boundaries:

> It was the day, what time the powerful moon >
> Makes the poor Bankside creature wet its shoon, >
> In its own hall . . .

The other characteristic is a marked tendency towards parenthesis; that is, the turning-aside from the main argument to pursue some subordinate theme. This turning-aside is usually marked by brackets at the opening and the closing of the parenthesis:

> when these (in worthy scorn >
> Of those, that put out monies, on return >
> From Venice, Paris, or some inland passage >
> Of six times to, and fro, without embassage, >
> Or him that backward went to Berwick, or which >
> Did dance the famous Morris, unto Norwich) . . .

Without the parenthesis, the argument would read:

> It was the day, what time the powerful moon
> Makes the poor Bankside creature wet its shoon,
> In its own hall; when these

> At Bread Street's Mermaid having dined, and merry,
> Proposed to go to Holborn in a wherry.

The parenthesis puts the reader aside from the main theme, but it also brings the reader back, and that is a characteristic of the second variety of heroic couplet.

A master of this variety was perhaps the most neglected poet of any importance in English, William Chamberlayne (1619–89). It may well be his tendency towards parenthesis, and parenthesis within parenthesis, accompanied by a very free handling of enjambment, that has brought about this neglect. But these characteristics are apposite to his theme, which is the fantastic set of adventures undergone by the knight Argalia and his love, Pharonnida. The characteristics in question are also apposite to Chamberlayne's style, which is an admixture of beauty with strangeness.

Here is an extract from Chamberlayne's long poem *Pharonnida*. The present author has taken the liberty of marking in bold type with (and) the opening and closing of the main parentheses, and with [and] the opening and closing of those subordinate parentheses contained within the main ones. Pharonnida is dreaming of a future life with her lover:

> Whilst thus enthean fire did lie concealed
> With different curtains, (lest, [by being revealed,]
> Cross fate, [which could not quench it,] should to death
> Scorch all their hopes, burned in the angry breath
> Of her incensed father) – whilst the fair
> Pharonnida was striving to repair
> The wakeful ruins of the day, (within
> Her bed, [whose down of late by love had been
> Converted into thorns],) she (having paid
> The restless tribute of her sorrow), staid
> To breathe awhile in broken slumbers, (such
> As with short blasts cool feverish brains; [but much

> More was in hers]) – A strong pathetic dream,
> (Diverting by enigmas Nature's stream,
> [Long hovering through the portals of her mind
> On vain phantastic wings],) at length did find
> The glimmerings of obstructed reason by
> A brighter beam of pure divinity . . .

('Enthean', by the way, is a rare word meaning 'inspired by an indwelling god'.) There is no reason, other than time and space, to stop quoting at this point. The sentence continues for several more lines in which, as in the ones already quoted, each idea gives rise to other ideas, and parenthesis grows out of parenthesis.

That forgotten master strongly influenced the poet who perhaps was the most notable exponent of this parenthetical variety of couplet: John Keats (1795–1821). He goes one step further than Chamberlayne, in that his sense hardly ever matches up with the rhyme scheme of the couplet. Thus, to the tendency towards parenthesis, and the persistent enjambment, Keats adds the effect of directing the sense not with the couplet, as one would find in Pope, but against it. The following passage, from 'Lamia', begins, therefore, in mid-couplet, seeming to ignore the tendency of the rhyme. Lamia, a snake who has the superficial appearance of a woman, is making preparations for her bridal feast. The style, extravagant and exotic, matches its arcane subject:

> She set herself, (high-thoughted,) how to dress
> The misery in fit magnificence.
> She did so, but 'tis doubtful how and whence
> Came, and who were her subtle servitors.
> About the halls, and to and from the doors,
> There was a noise of wings, till (in short space)
> The glowing banquet-room shone with wide-arched grace;
> A haunting music, (sole [perhaps] and lone
> Supportress of the fairy-roof) made moan
> Throughout, (as fearful the whole charm might fade).

The passage finishes, as it began, in mid-couplet. The whole metre is very plastic, with its run-on sentences, its loose syntax, its refusal to be contained within the couplet form. Nevertheless, the chime of the couplets is heard as a kind of counterpoint to the sense, and it is in this way that a modern poet would use this metre. The modern poet would, on the whole, prefer the Keatsian to the Popeian variety of couplet.

The present author, meditating on the threatened loss of his eyesight, quite instinctively utilized this freer mode of couplet in a poem called 'The Good Doctor':

> Doctor, the nurses fly you. That quick flash
> Of wit or spectacles would pink the flesh
> Of blonde Miss Winfield or the tub of lard
> You had before her, as it scores my hide.
> For I flinch too, and 'Steady now' you say
> Thrusting a lump of coke into my eye
> (At least it feels like coke) 'you need control.'
> I do indeed, if I'm to blink at will,
> Flex the eye muscles, peer into the sun,
> And take my painful medicine like a man.
> 'Mere sensation,' you say – but how it sears,
> My vision, subject to your probes and flares!
> And yet you are a good doctor. I was blind,
> You gave me sight, mapped the scar-tissue, stemmed
> The blood that wept behind my retina,
> Fading my townscape green. Every cure
> Is moral victory on the optic plane,
> And how you, solemn doctor, laughed again
> When I deciphered words a child could tell
> From your illuminated board. Will?
> Perhaps – perhaps encouraged. Maybe I saw
> Because there was someone to see, someone to care.

This not only goes in for enjambment and parenthesis but utilizes pararhyme, the nature of which will be defined in the next chapter. Yet the metre here would certainly be considered formal compared with much verse of the later twentieth century.

It will be assumed from the foregoing argument that the heroic couplet, both in its Popeian and in its Keatsian varieties, is capable of range and flexibility. The reason why it lost ground steadily to blank verse is that it is only partially capable of dramatic effect. If we return to the couplet as used by Dryden, we shall be able to recognize both its virtues and its limitations.

There is no doubt that Dryden was a heroic poet. His translation of the *Aeneid* in couplets is far superior to that of Surrey in blank verse. The point can be readily made if we look at Dryden's version of the same passage as was quoted at the beginning of the previous chapter in the version of Surrey. Dryden has:

> All were attentive to the godlike man,
> When from his lofty couch he thus began:
> 'Great queen, what you command me to relate
> Renews the sad remembrance of our fate:
> An empire from its old foundations rent
> And every woe the Trojans underwent . . . '

This is crisp and business-like, and was famous in its time – as the *Paradise Lost* of John Milton most certainly was not. Why, then, did taste in narrative move away from the heroic couplet of Dryden and towards the blank verse of Milton?

The answer can be seen if we look at Dryden's plays. He made attempt after attempt at heroic tragedy, but these efforts cannot be acted now. They may sustain an isolated speech, like the one from *Aurung-Zebe*, quoted at the beginning of this chapter. But it is when they seek to render dialogue that the limitations of heroic couplets, at least in their Popeian variety, make themselves felt.

In the first scene of *The Conquest of Granada*, the Moorish families, Zegry and Abencerrago, confront each other in warlike posture:

HAMET   'Tis not for fear the combat we refuse,
          But we our gained advantage will not lose.
ZULEMA   In combating, but two of you will fall;
          And we resolve we will despatch you all.
OZMYN   We'll double yet the exchange before we die,
          And each of ours two lives of yours shall buy.

(ALMANZOR *enters betwixt them, as they stand ready to engage.*)

ALMANZOR I cannot stay to ask which cause is best;
          But this is so to me, because opprest.

Almanzor, a stranger to the conflicting parties, instinctively joins the weaker side. However, there is a dichotomy between the would-be heroic activity and the pernickety numbering of the factions: 'but two of you will fall', 'We'll double yet the exchange'. This mock-precision or gesticulation towards wit seems to be latent in this variety of the couplet, and produces an effect at variance with the posturing. One can only say that the action would have been happier in blank verse.

Is the heroic tragedy capable of revival now? Ostensibly, it would seem not. Yet there have been attempts to translate its counterpart, the formal comedy of the French playwright Molière (1622–73), into couplets. The most brilliant of these is that of Richard Wilbur (b. 1921). Here is M. Orgon, back from the country, being told sad news of his wife but remaining besotted with his favourite, Tartuffe, after whom the play in question is named:

ORGON   Has all been well, these two days I've been gone?
          How are the family? What's been going on?
DORINE   Your wife, two days ago, had a bad fever,
          And a fierce headache that refused to leave her.

ORGON   Ah. And Tartuffe?

DORINE   Tartuffe? Why, he's round and red,
Bursting with health, and excellently fed.

ORGON   Poor fellow!

DORINE   That night the mistress was unable
To take a single bite at the dinner table.
Her headache-pains, she said, were simply hellish.

ORGON   Ah. And Tartuffe?

DORINE   He ate his meal with relish.
And zealously devoured in her presence
A leg of mutton and a brace of pheasants.

This suggests that the Popeian couplet is still alive for satiric purposes. It would, however, take a very unusual talent to employ the old form as adroitly as this, and the result might be more peculiar than poetic. Wilbur's rhymes are certainly more far-fetched than any Dryden and Pope would have approved, and this is necessary to maintain flexibility: 'fever'/'leave her'; 'presence'/'pheasants'. There is also a degree of indecorum in the diction: 'simply hellish' is a 1920s kind of middle-class slang.

Such liberties as these are probably necessary if any version of the couplet is to be used in modern times. Peter Porter (b. 1929), perhaps the dominant satirical poet in mid-century Britain, has a similar fund of resource in adopting the metre. His rhythm is freer than that of Wilbur. While his are undoubtedly couplets, one could use the term 'heroic' only with a degree of qualification. Porter does indeed set up an iambic norm in the opening lines. But he then proceeds to flout that norm by adding lightly stressed and medium-lightly stressed syllables, to the extent that some lines could only dubiously be scanned as pentameters. It creates a kind of lurching effect, very much at one with the theme of 'Made in Heaven'. This is a scathing satire on the débutante who marries for prestige and money, much as she would be tempted by goods displayed in the then fashionable stores, Heals and Harrods:

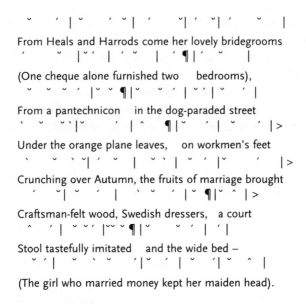

From Heals and Harrods come her lovely bridegrooms

(One cheque alone furnished two   bedrooms),

From a pantechnicon   in the dog-paraded street

Under the orange plane leaves,   on workmen's feet

Crunching over Autumn, the fruits of marriage brought

Craftsman-felt wood, Swedish dressers,   a court

Stool tastefully imitated   and the wide bed –

(The girl who married money kept her maiden head).

This is a swashbuckling rhythm, always threatening to turn into hexameters; that is to say, six-stress lines. But, for a number of reasons, hexameters are always unstable in English, and little of merit has been written in them. In any case, there is a basic five-stress rhythm pulsing through this poem. It is established in the opening lines, and sustained by providing extra syllables of medium-light (rather than medium) stress.

This loose (rather than rough) five-stress rhythm is in the tradition of a number of past satirists, masters of invective, such as John Donne (1572–1631) and John Marston (?1575–1634). The latter, indeed, Peter Porter has celebrated as an exemplar in a satirical poem appreciably finer than the one which has just been quoted, effective though that is. But 'John Marston Advises Anger' is written not in couplets, but in Porter's own highly individual blank verse. This suggests that, even for satire in modern times, metre in couplets has limited possibilities.

If the Keatsian couplet survives to an extent, the Popeian variety has gone, probably for ever. Its formality cannot accommodate the indecorous speech patterns of our time without putting the language under a measure of constraint. Any attempt in that direction would be likely to look as though it were pastiche. The style would echo previous practitioners too obviously, and be an invocation of the past rather than a voice emanating from the present. It therefore follows that what affects the couplet in our period also variegates use, in any metre, of rhyme.

4

RHYME AND PARARHYME

Rhyme is the exact echoing of a sound at the end of one line by the sound at the end of another line. We have already seen how this operates in the heroic couplet, where each new set of rhymes is designated with a new letter of the alphabet:

When I consider life, 'tis all a cheat;	a
Yet, fooled with hope, men favour the deceit;	a
Trust on, and think tomorrow will repay;	b
Tomorrow's false than the former day	b

and so on.

The same denotation applies to all rhymes in whatever order they come. Apart from the area of verse covered by the heroic couplet, probably the most successful form in which rhyme is employed is the lyric. Francis Turner Palgrave in *The Golden Treasury*, a Victorian anthology devoted to the genre, defined the lyric as a short poem, turning on a single thought or situation. One can differentiate within this category, from the lyric proper, the song-lyric. This latter has the quality of seeming as though composed to be sung. Its language tends to be euphonious; melodic, and pleasing to the ear.

Some of the best song-lyrics ever written occurred in the time of Shakespeare. In fact, it was Shakespeare who composed many of them. A fine example is the dirge in *Cymbeline*. It begins:

Fear no more the heat o' the sun,	a
Nor the furious winter's rages;	b
Thou thy worldly task hast done,	a
Home art gone and ta'en thy wages.	b
Golden lads and girls all must,	c
As chimney-sweepers come to dust.	c

This appears to be simplicity itself, but appearance can be deceptive. The poem has had a far-reaching influence. Well after Shakespeare's time, the playwright James Shirley (1596–1666), in his *Contention of Ajax and Ulysses*, picked up something of the same music. One has a sense of the voice dropping at the end of the line, at the end of the sentence, at the end of the set of verses:

The glories of our blood and state	a
Are shadows, not substantial things;	b
There is no armour against fate;	a
Death lays his icy hand on kings.	b
Sceptre and crown	c
Must tumble down,	c
And in the dust be equal made	d
With the poor crooked scythe and spade.	d

The 'set of verses' referred to is a stanza; that is to say, a group of lines with a set metrical form and rhyme scheme, recurring as a group through a given poem. Thus, the first stanza just quoted gives rise to a second and a third stanza, of equivalent metric structure and rhyme. Here is the third (and final) stanza. The notation of rhyme begins afresh with each set of verses; a b a b, and so on:

The garlands wither on your brow,	a
Then boast no more your mighty deeds;	b
Upon death's purple altar now,	a
See where the victor-victim bleeds.	b
Your heads must come	c
To the cold tomb;	c
Only the actions of the just	d
Smell sweet and blossom in their dust.	d

There are rhythmic variations on the basic ground of the metre, and these could be pointed out. But these variations are slight compared with the diversification found in dramatic blank verse, or even the heroic couplet of satiric poetry,

The lyric word-music (for that is what it amounts to) revived, after a period of attenuation, in the Romantic upsurge of the late eighteenth century. This was heralded by William Blake (1757–1827), who took notice of Shakespearian lyric at a time when it was generally undervalued:

Ah, Sun-flower! weary of time,	a
Who countest the steps of the Sun:	b
Seeking after that sweet golden clime	a
Where the traveller's journey is done;	b
Where the Youth pined away with desire,	a
And the pale Virgin shrouded in snow:	b
Arise from their graves and aspire	a
Where my Sun-flower wishes to go.	b

One stanza mimics the other. The rhythm is very near its basic metre; in this case, anapaestic trimeter. The diction – the language of the poetry – is simple, and appears capable of being set to music, whether it is in the end sung or not. A related poem, 'The Chimney Sweeper', begins:

When my mother died I was very young,	a
And my father sold me while yet my tongue	a

Could scarcely cry 'weep weep weep weep,'   b
So your chimneys I sweep & in soot I sleep.   b

There's little Tom Dacre, who cried when his head   a
That curled like a lamb's back, was shaved, so I said   a
'Hush Tom never mind it, for when your head's bare,   b
You know that the soot cannot spoil your white hair.'   b

These are couplets, but their tendency is different from anything instanced in the previous chapter. Almost everything here pertains to song. The topic may be sad, but it is treated as an occasion for melody.

This does not mean that song-lyrics necessarily require to be sung. The dirge in *Cymbeline*, when that play is staged, is customarily spoken. It is true that Shirley's 'The glories of our blood and state' was sung when *The Contention of Ajax and Ulysses* was produced. But that dramatic debate has long since vanished from the theatre. Its most famous song survives as a piece for poetry recitals, plangently recorded (for example) by the late Cecil Trouncer.

The fact of the matter is that a song-lyric has a melody of its own, to which the art of the composer can only superadd. Often he clogs the sense in so doing, and sometimes he finds it necessary to wrench the rhythm about. So it is the lighter and slighter song-lyrics that tend to be set to music successfully. There is this song-lyric by A. E. Housman (1859–1936):

With rue my heart is laden   a
   For golden friends I had,   b
For many a rose-lipt maiden   a
   And many a lightfoot lad.   b

By brooks too broad for leaping,   a
   The lightfoot boys are laid;   b
The rose-lipt girls are sleeping   a
   In fields where roses fade.   b

The poem has been set to music successfully, but there is precious little content here. One has only to compare this charming trifle with what Blake made of Shakespeare's 'Fear no more the heat of the sun'. Blake's 'Youth pined away with desire' is a presentation of pain and frustration; Housman's 'lightfoot lad' is, by comparison, insubstantial. Even the 'rue' with which the speaker's 'heart' is 'laden' comes straight out of the mad scene of Ophelia in *Hamlet* – without, it would seem, much of an emotional intermediary, or correlative. The inference would be that a good song-lyric stands on its own feet. It is the weaker song-lyrics that need the support of a music from outside.

The question is one of density in language. It has often been suggested that the diction of Donne is rough, possibly through lack of craft. But Donne's diction varies with his topic. He can produce a formal lyric, exquisitely polished, about his necessary departure from his wife on a voyage. Here is the first stanza. The rhymes tend to alternate, a b a b. That is quite usual, in song-lyric:

Sweetest love, I do not go	a
For weariness of thee,	b
Nor in hope the world can show	a
A fitter love for me;	b
But since that I	c
Must die at last, 'tis best	d
To use myself in jest	d
Thus by feigned deaths to die.	c

This is a suggestion of song rather than song itself. As is the case with the dirge in *Cymbeline*, this poem will be recognized on frequentation as being more complex than it seemed at first acquaintance. That dying 'by feigned deaths' is an idea that could well be lost if sung, rather than spoken with a due regard for sense. Further, like the lyrics of Shakespeare and of Blake, it has a distinctive rhythm; metrical, certainly, but individual nonetheless.

Donne's so-called 'rough' rhythms occur when he increases

his dramatic content to suggest the nuances of the speaking voice. At this point, he will be found to be writing not song-lyric, but lyric proper.

Consider Donne's lyric 'The Sun Rising'. Two lovers lie in bed, and the male addresses the sun with familiarity, wishing to be left alone with his partner. The first stanza goes:

Busy old fool, unruly sun,	a
Why dost thou thus	b
Through windows, and through curtains, call on us?	b
Must to thy motions lovers' seasons run?	a
Saucy pedantic wretch, go chide	c
Late school-boys and sour prentices,	d
Go tell court-huntsmen, that the King will ride,	e
Call country aunts to harvest offices;	d
Love, all alike, no season knows, nor clime,	f
Nor hours, days, months, which are the rags of time.	f

The rhyme scheme is more irregular than any we have looked at so far, and the stanza is more extended in form. The b-rhymes, 'thus' and 'us', almost match up with the d-rhymes, 'prentices' and 'offices'. This lyric seems designed to accommodate the speaking voice. The effect approaches, but does not circumscribe, that of drama. Certainly, in the lyrics of Donne there is a degree of spoken invocation; somebody is being addressed. In this instance, with a spirit of mockery, it is the sun.

In 'A Nocturnal upon St Lucy's Day', a poem mourning the death of a woman much loved, the object of address is an audience composed of younger and less experienced lovers. Here is the first stanza:

'Tis the year's midnight, and it is the day's,	a
Lucy's, who scarce seven hours herself unmasks,	b
The sun is spent, and now his flasks	b
Send forth light squibs, no constant rays;	a

> The world's whole sap is sunk: c
> The general balm th' hydroptic earth has drunk,   c
> Whither, as to the bed's feet, life is shrunk,   c
> Dead and interred; yet all these seem to laugh   d
> Compared with me, who am their epitaph.   d

Again, there is an extended stanza. But notice that Donne does not repeat the rhyme scheme that he had used in 'The Sun Rising'. Indeed, as the stanza proceeds, the metre accommodates itself to a series of coupled (rather than alternating) rhymes. This takes the mode further away from song and nearer to a formalized drama, a kind of meditation that is near-satiric. Even so, there is an element of strain; a kind of tension between form and language. One may concede that there is nothing in the stanza which cannot be glossed or explained. 'Flasks' are the stars, which store up the sun's energy as flasks store gunpowder. 'Light squibs' are weak flashes of light. But these are not, perhaps, the best possible words. The meaning arises out of the need to rhyme; the rhymes do not altogether arise out of the meaning.

Similar elaboration, and a similar tension between form and language, can be found in the work of one who is ostensibly a dissimilar poet, John Keats. 'Ode to a Nightingale' is, like most of Keats's best poems, a meditation on poetry. In this case, the nightingale plays the role of muse, or inspiration. The poem begins with the portrayal of a condition familiar to most writers, a kind of melancholy associated with occlusion, specifically 'writer's block'. An opiate is a narcotic drug, of which an extract made from hemlock is only one variety. Lethe in Greek mythology was the river of forgetfulness, of which the dead drank in order to lose all sense of their former life. A dryad is a spirit of the wood to whom offerings could be made. This poem may be presumed to be one such offering:

> My heart aches, and a drowsy numbness pains   a
>   My sense, as though of hemlock I had drunk,   b

Or emptied some dull opiate to the drains	a
One minute past, and Lethe-wards had sunk:	b
'Tis not through envy of thy happy lot,	c
But being too happy in thy happiness, –	d
That thou, light-winged Dryad of the trees,	e
In some melodious plot	c
Of beechen green, and shadows numberless,	d
Singest of summer in full-throated ease.	e

The control over syntax in the stanza is impressive, as anyone may find out by trying to emulate the poet's form of verse. One has to admire his negotiation of the tricky c-rhymes, 'lot' and 'plot'.

As the poem evolves, however, an underlying strain becomes perceptible. Keats maintains his rhyme scheme, the difficult a b a b c d e c d e, until the end. But, by the end, it is possible to point to words chosen for reason of rhyme rather than reason of meaning:

Forlorn! the very word is like a bell	a
To toll me back from thee to my sole self!	b
Adieu! the fancy cannot cheat so well	a
As she is famed to do, deceiving elf.	b
Adieu! adieu! thy plaintive anthem fades	c
Past the near meadows, over the still stream,	d
Up the hill-side; and now 'tis buried deep	e
In the next valley-glades:	c
Was it a vision, or a waking dream?	d
Fled is that music: – do I wake or sleep?	e

The word 'self' is not necessarily the best word to use if the poet has already got across the sense of solitariness. Its partner in the b-rhyme is by no means the best word to use as a means of representing 'fancy'. An elf is an inferior sort of fairy, malign and usually stunted in growth. Such an ascription may be felt as somewhat demeaning. At any rate, the 'fancy'/'elf' parallel hardly enhances what has long been thought one of the finest poems in the language.

This elaborate stanza form of Keats, like that of Donne, probably owes its inception to the example of the Italian canzone, whose greatest master was Petrarch (1304–74). The canzone is an elaborately rhymed poem, written in stanzas, each with the same rhyme scheme throughout. Whatever stanza is chosen can have anything between seven and twenty lines, and it is no easy matter to repeat this multi-rhymed form through the length of a poem.

The canzone was imitated by some of the Elizabethans, but characteristically they did not lay too much conceptual weight upon the form. Donne, with his intense meditative form of lyric, was an exception. We have seen how at times he put his language under strain in order to accomplish his metrical form. We have seen how Keats felt the strain as well. The fact of the matter is that English has far fewer rhymes than Italian. It is therefore difficult to achieve an unforced lyricism without having to overcome a tension between form and language. The language is liable to become distorted.

Weaker poets than Donne and Keats tend to fall into obsolete phrases, a kind of willed archaism technically known as poetic diction. The eighteenth century is usually held to be guilty of this, but far worse instances may be found in *The Oxford Book of English Verse* edited by Sir Arthur Quiller-Couch. For example, consider the linguistic deformations of the following – the numbers are those by which Quiller-Couch designates the poems in his anthology: 'Laughing maids, unstaying,/Deeming it trick-playing' (745); 'Is she nested? Does she kneel/In the twilight stilly?' (746); 'All the way by which I drew anear' (878). Some of those perpetrating such atrophies of language were competent writers in their day. But the disciplines of full rhyme and formal metre proved to be too much for their craft.

Yet there was a way out of this tension between form and language. It was hinted in the partial rhymes of Donne. He has sets of rhymes which are related, but which do not exactly follow one another. This congruence may be seen in the stanza already quoted from 'The Sun Rising', where 'thus' and 'us' occur in proximity with 'prentices' and 'offices'. It may also be seen in Keats's 'Nightingale', where 'happiness' and 'numberless' abut on 'trees' and 'ease'.

Neither Donne nor Keats uses these near-rhyming effects systematically. But Keats, at any rate, was the prime influence on a twentieth-century poet who, though no metrical innovator in other respects, brought partial rhyme into the centre of the English poetic tradition. Wilfred Owen (1893–1918) was killed in the First World War, at the same age as his master, Keats, who had died of tuberculosis. Whereas Keats's subject was poetry, that of Owen, as might have been expected, was war. He adapts the sensuousness and luxuriance of Keats to this rigorous theme.

An early poem, 'Leaves from my Diary', begins:

Leaves
  Murmuring by myriads in the shimmering trees.
Lives
  Wakening with wonder in the Pyrenees.
Birds
  Cheerily chirping in the early day.
Bards
  Singing of summer scything thro' the hay.

Here we have an alternation of full rhymes – 'trees', 'Pyrenees' – with partial rhymes – 'Leaves', 'Lives'.

In Owen's achieved style, this use of partial rhyme is even more striking. The following is the start of one of his best poems, 'Exposure'. It is a kind of composite monologue, spoken by the half-frozen men in the trenches, waiting for the action to begin:

> Our brains ache, in the merciless iced east winds that knive us . . .
> Wearied we keep awake because the night is silent . . .
> Low, drooping flares confuse our memory of the salient . . .
> Worried by silence, sentries whisper, curious, nervous,
> > But nothing happens.

The last line in each stanza is unrhymed. But what of the 'rhymes' used in the other lines? They have been called 'partial', but that makes them sound as though they were in some way a mistake, rather than, as they are, an achievement. The technical term is pararhyme. This is one of the key ways out of the slavery to full rhyme which has limited so much verse in the past, and in some cases done violence to the language.

Owen's pararhyme is characteristically of a special kind, whereby the consonants of the rhyme relate to each other, as in their turn the vowels do. Thus 'knive us' and 'nervous' alliterate as well as assonate; that is to say, the consonants echo, as well as vowels.

This usage has had an influence far more widely spread than is generally recognized. If we call 'knive us'/'nervous' a three-quarter rhyme, the rhyme scheme of 'Exposure' can be annotated as follows. The second stanza runs:

> Watching, we hear the mad gusts tugging on the wire,   a
> Like twitching agonies of men among its brambles.   b
> Northward, incessantly, the flickering gunnery rumbles,   ¾b
> Far off, like a dull rumour of some other war.   ¾a
> > What are we doing here?   c

The last line must be taken as blank, that is to say unrhymed. One could argue that it part-rhymes with 'wire', but there is no other instance in the poem of the final line of a stanza part-rhyming with any preceding lines. Furthermore, for 'here' to part-rhyme with 'wire' and 'war' would be to break Owen's convention – that the consonants of the two rhyme words, as well as the vowels, have to relate.

The most remarkable instance of pararhyme in Owen derives not from the canzone-effects of Keats, but from Keats's blank verse. This, by reason of choice of vocabulary, and word repetition, achieves a considerable degree of euphony. An influential example is a passage in *The Fall of Hyperion*, when a poet encounters his muse:

'None can usurp this height', returned that shade,
'But those to whom the miseries of the world
Are misery, and will not let them rest.
All else who find a haven in the world,
Where they may thoughtless sleep away their days,
If by a chance into this fane they come,
Rot on the pavement where thou rotted'st half.'

('Fane is an archaic word for 'temple' or 'shrine'.) This is so rich in sound that one tends to remember it as rhyming rather than as blank verse. It is, therefore, by no great feat of transmutation that Owen turns its music into pararhyme in his most famous poem, 'Strange Meeting'. Here a soldier addresses his enemy, killed in battle:

'None,' said that other, 'save the undone years,   a
The hopelessness. Whatever hope is yours,   ¾a
Was my life also; I went hunting wild   b
After the wildest beauty in the world,   ¾b
Which lies not calm in eyes or braided hair,   c
But mocks the steady running of the hour,   ¾c
And if it grieves, grieves richlier than here.'   ¾c

The agreement of consonants, as well as vowels, has been very consciously followed by W. H. Auden (1907–73) in *Paid on Both Sides*, his condensed drama of a conflict between two rival tribes. He seems to see tribalism as endemic in human nature and projects that stoical view through a chorus:

Outside on frozen soil lie armies killed	a
Who seem familiar but they are cold.	¾a
How the most solid wish he tries to keep	b
His hands show through; he never will look up,	½b
Say 'I am good'. On him misfortune falls	c
More than enough. Better where no one feels . . .	¾c

This attention to echo effects in consonants has not, on the whole, been taken up by later poets. The characteristic usage in pararhyme is not three-quarter rhyme, but half-rhyme and quarter-rhyme. Quite often this is intermingled with full rhyme, to secure a varying grade of emphasis. Many of the best-known poets of the twentieth century employ this hybrid pattern. W. B. Yeats (1865–1939) was a master of stanzaic form. He does not deploy pararhyme so systematically as Owen. But there is no doubt that he liberally intermixes pararhyme with full rhyme. By this means, he manages to combine a characteristic resonance with what seems to be an inherent speakability. In 'Among Schoolchildren' he sees himself as a battered old creature who still has in him the youth he once treasured. The poem begins:

I walk through the long schoolroom questioning;	a
A kind old nun in a white hood replies;	b
The children learn to cipher and to sing,	a
To study reading-books and histories,	½b
To cut and sew, be neat in everything	a
In the best modern way – the children's eyes	b
In momentary wonder stare upon	c
A sixty-year-old smiling public man.	½c

Even with the apparently full a-rhyme, the ˘-stress of the '-ing' in 'questioning' in reality only part-rhymes with the ´-stress of 'sing', and neither fully rhymes with the ^-stress of the '-ing' in 'every-thing'. This pitting of an apparently full rhyme on one unequally stressed syllable against another is a characteristic Yeats effect.

Something of the sort may be found in many other twentieth-century poems.

A distinguished example is 'Church Going' by Philip Larkin (1922–85). The churchgoer in question is a young agnostic entering a church as an act of inquisitiveness. In spite of himself, he becomes impressed with a sense of tradition:

Once I am sure there's nothing going on	a
I step inside, letting the door thud shut.	b
Another church: matting, seats and stone,	½a
And little books; sprawlings of flowers, cut	b
For Sunday, brownish now; some brass and stuff	c
Up at the holy end; the small neat organ;	¼a
And a tense, musty, unignorable silence,	d
Brewed God knows how long. Hatless, I take off	½c
My cycle-clips in awkward reverence.	½d

There is one pair of full rhymes, 'shut' and 'cut'. But the vowel is short, and end-stopped; that is to say, it ends with a consonant. The effect is subdued, and this subdued quality is quietened even further by the presence of other quiet and end-stopped sounds: 'stuff' and 'off', for instance. 'On' is a fairly quiet word in itself. It half-rhymes with 'stone', which is more resonant, but quarter-rhymes with 'organ'. This is an example of part-rhyming on unequal stress. The organ is small and, manifestly, is not playing. Its modesty is enacted through the restraint of the verse in which it is presented.

The second stanza gains a little in confidence. The speaker moves forward into the church, and begins – tentatively, it may be – to touch the font, the lectern, the Bible. There are two pairs of full rhymes in this stanza: 'new'/'few'; 'door'/'for'. But these are not the most resonant of sounds. They are surrounded, moreover, by pararhymes. One of these, 'pronounce'/'sixpence', is very subdued indeed; a quarter-rhyme on unequally stressed syllables.

As the poem goes on, however, the confidence increases and the rhymes, correspondingly, become fuller. There are three sets of full rhymes in the third stanza, four in the fourth and fifth stanzas, while the last two stanzas are completely rhymed and, further, much more resonant in their basic vowel sounds:

A serious house on serious earth it is,	a
In whose blent air all our compulsions meet,	b
Are recognised, and robed as destinies.	a
And that much never can be obsolete,	b
Since someone will forever be surprising	c
A hunger in himself to be more serious,	a
And gravitating with it to this ground	d
Which, he once heard, was proper to grow wise in,	c
If only that so many dead lie round.	d

Not only is this stanza more fully rhymed than its predecessors, but those rhymes are on more resonant vowels: 'surprising', 'rising'; 'ground', 'round'. There are internal rhymes; rhymes, that is to say, occurring within the line: '*for*ever'/ *more*; 'some*one*'/ '*hun*ger'. These, in their turn, increase the resonance.

The diction, too, helps. From the naturalistic and almost furtive details of the first two stanzas we move on to higher levels of diction. In this last stanza, there are phrases such as 'all our compulsions' and 'robed as destinies'. These create a sense of aspiration which is the note on which the poem ends. As Oliver Goldsmith (?1730–74) has it, in his poem *The Deserted Village*, 'Fools, who came to scoff, remained to pray'. That is in some way an eighteenth-century counterpart of Larkin's 'Church Going'.

But aspiration is not a trait much found in modern verse. A more satirical use of pararhyme, some forty years after the death of Owen, comes from Peter Porter. We looked at one of his poems in the previous chapter. Much of the colloquial ease of 'Metamorphosis', another poem about thwarted love, comes from the fact that he is able to gauge the extent of pararhyme he wishes to

use. He is not tied down, as so many previous poets were, to the
clanging of unvaried full rhyme:

This new Daks suit, greeny-brown,	a
Oyster coloured buttons, single vent, tapered	b
Trousers, no waistcoat, hairy tweed – my own:	½a
A suit to show responsibility, to show	c
Return to life – easily got for two pounds down,	a
Paid off in six months – the first stage in the change.	⅛b
I am only the image I can force upon the town.	a
The town will have me: I stalk in glass,	a
A thin reflection in the windows, best	b
In jewellers' velvet backgrounds – I don't pass,	a
I stop, elect to look at wedding rings –	c
My figure filled with clothes, my putty mask,	½a
A face fragrant with arrogance, stuffed	⅛b
With recognition – I am myself at last.	½a
I wait in the pub with my Worthington.	a
Then you come in – how many days did love have,	b
How can they all be catalogued again?	½a
We talk of how we miss each other – I tell	c
Some truth – You, cruel stories built of men:	½a
'It wasn't good at first, but he's improving'.	⅛b
More talk about his car, his drinks, his friends.	½a
I look to the wild mirror at the bar –	a
A beautiful girl smiles beside me – she's real	b
And her regret is real. If only I had a car,	a
If only – my stately self cringes, renders down;	c
As in a werewolf film I'm horrible, far	a
Below the collar – my fingers crack, my tyrant suit	⅛b
Chokes me as it hugs me in its fire.	½a

The eighth-rhyme in the last stanza of 'real' and 'suit' is disputable. It would not seem to be any kind of a rhyme out of context. But a pattern has been set up in previous stanzas, whereby the fourth line is blank and the sixth line faintly echoes the second. The important thing to notice is that the first, third, fifth and seventh lines of each stanza carry the fuller rhymes.

There is an expressive function here. It is the converse of what we found in 'Church Going'. The speaker is reasonably confident in the first stanza, and there is a fuller set of rhymes to show this: 'brown', 'own', 'down', town', By the third and fourth stanzas, he is dwindling in substance. The b-rhymes are wheezier, in so far as they rhyme at all: 'have'/'improving'; 'real'/'suit'. In particular, the a-rhyme, which elsewhere in the poem we could depend upon, in the final line fails to rhyme fully with the previous a-rhymes – 'bar', 'car', 'far' – because the fine brown suit has consumed its owner in its 'fire'.

It is a remarkable fact that young and amateur poets do not take more notice of this door of pararhyme that has been opened to them. Most of the great poets this century do not, as the popular fallacy has it, abandon rhyme and metre. But their rhyme tends to be of the kind illustrated in this chapter, so that they are able to build degrees of emphasis into their verse. They are able, also, to avoid something of the war between metre and sense from which their predecessors to some extent suffered.

5

SPRUNG VERSE

Gerard Manley Hopkins (1844–89) was the first to name a phenomenon called sprung verse or sprung rhythm. His theory regarding the matter is found in the Preface he intended to affix to his *Collected Poems*. However, these were not issued in his lifetime nor, indeed, until 1918.

Hopkins declared that every foot had one principal stress and that the other syllables were more or less lightly stressed. Sprung rhythm was measured by feet of from one to four syllables, and for particular effects any number of light syllables might be used. The lightest of these could be termed outrides, which were virtually weightless syllables added to a given foot. These need not be counted in the scansion, on the grounds that the weight of stress would be almost negligible.

Any two stresses might follow one another consecutively or else be divided by one, two or three light syllables. There could be reversed feet, known as 'inversions', whereby a sequence of ˘ ´ might be turned into one of ´ ˘, or vice versa. If such reversal were to be repeated in two consecutive feet, it would superimpose a new rhythm on the original one. But since the original rhythm would not be forgotten, two rhythms could be apparent at one and the same time, in a kind of counterpoint. There could also be a pause, as in music, standing in lieu of a stress. That pause could be in excess of the unmarked caesura which would normally take place, or in addition to it. Several additions could be made to the theory that Hopkins put forward. There are a number of self-contradictions and obscurities. But, in the main, this is the theory of sprung rhythm.

What Hopkins has described here is, however, the manner in which the rhythm of English verse, when effective, has always proceeded. So, far from being an innovator, he pointed to a traditional process of verse which his own period, and that of the early twentieth century which succeeded it, was in danger of forgetting.

In 1879 Hopkins began a tragedy based on the life of St Winefred, of which fragments only remain. One of these is a chorus, designed as a kind of duet between the Leaden Echo, betokening negative attitudes, and the Golden Echo, betokening hope. The part spoken by the Leaden Echo runs as follows:

> How to keep – is there any any, is there none such,
>   nowhere known some, bow or brooch or braid
>   or brace, lace, latch or catch or key to keep
> Back beauty, keep it, beauty, beauty, beauty, . . . from
>   vanishing away?
> O is there no frowning of these wrinkles, rankëd
>   wrinkles deep,
> Down? no waving off of these most mournful messengers,
>   still messengers, sad and stealing messengers of grey?
> No there's none, there's none, O no there's none,
> Nor can you long be, what you now are, called fair,
> Do what you may do, what, do what you may,
> And wisdom is early to despair:
> Be beginning; since, no, nothing can be done

To keep at bay
Age and age's evils, hoar hair,
Ruck and wrinkle, drooping, dying, death's worst, winding
   sheets, tombs and worms and tumbling to decay;
So be beginning, be beginning to despair.
O there's none; no no no there's none:
Be beginning to despair, to despair,
Despair, despair, despair, despair.

This demands some skill in reading aloud. But if a reading is
rehearsed, the chorus will be found to make sense rhythmically
and indeed to be an engaging form of song-lyric.

The first line is a loose hexameter. The hexameter, as has already
been remarked, is a form of line unstable in English. It tends to
break up into its component parts, or in other ways to create
ambiguities as to how it is to be spoken. In this case, we have to
bear in mind Hopkins's own dictum that, first of all, a number
of extra light syllables can be superadded to the basic foot, and,
second, such syllables need not necessarily be counted in scansion.

Each foot is determined by a heavy stress. Since you cannot have
more than one heavy stress in a foot, the line will take shape for
speaker and critic alike when it is determined where the heavy
stresses are. This initial hexameter is followed by what is basically
a line with five heavy stresses, and it is mostly five-stress lines that
follow:

How to keep – is there any any, is there none such,

nowhere known some, bow or brooch or braid

or brace, lace, latch or catch or key to keep

Back beauty, keep it, beauty, beauty, beauty, . . . from

´ ˘ ˘ |

vanishing away?

There are some lengthened feet here; for example:

´ ˘ ˘ ˘ |

any any, is there . . .

and

´ ˘ ˘ ˘ |

bow or brooch or braid or brace . . .

These, however, present no problems if a reading is prefigured that involves one heavy stress followed by a scurrying effect of light ones. Each individual foot covers a good deal of ground, so to speak, and therefore the lighter syllables should be spoken rapidly.

In the same reading, full measure should be given to the heavy stresses, even though they are few in comparison with the light ones. That is because the heavy stresses basically determine the rhythm. Read in this way, the chorus will seem lyrical, almost song-like, in its appeal. It is, in fact, an attractive set of echo effects.

Its virtues will be recognized if Hopkins's original is compared with an attempt at rewriting it by T. Sturge Moore (1870–1944). Sturge Moore was a poet with an academic cast of mind. He was far less of a rhythmic virtuoso than a metrist, though some of his poems – notably 'To Silence' – still deserve attention. His recasting of Hopkins's measure, however, is leaden indeed:

How keep beauty? Is there any way?
Is there nowhere any means to have it stay?
Will no bow or brooch or braid,
Brace or lace
Latch or catch
Or key to lock the door lend aid
Before beauty vanishes away?
No, no, there's none,

Nor can you long be fair;
Soon your best is done,
Wisdom must be early to despair:
Look now for eye, hoar hair,
Winding sheets and tumbling to decay;
Even now today
Be beginning to despair,
Despair, despair.

The echo effects of the original are lost. The evocative presentation of old age – 'wrinkles, rankëd wrinkles deep' – has gone. So
has the elegaic 'no waving of these most mournful messengers'; the
inevitable signs of an ageing process that cannot be evaded. There
is a play on words, 'waving' and 'waiving', that goes for nothing in
Sturge Moore's version.

But Sturge Moore's version is metrical. One has to say that. It
sticks closely to the ground-plan, the blueprint. Moore stumbles
into a good deal of cliché, however, in so doing. 'Before beauty
vanishes away' is a poor substitute for 'keep it, beauty, beauty,
beauty . . . from vanishing away'. In sticking to the metre, Sturge
Moore has lost the rhythm. What is more, he has lost with rhythm
the peculiar urgency of the original poem. It is a dynamic we
associate with poetry; the impulse that moves it; and moves us in
so doing. Without such an impulse, poetry is liable to degenerate
into mere verse.

One of the predecessors of Hopkins was Donne. In fact, the
poets can be linked together, for their sensual detail and for the
concentration of their religious sense. First, an extract from 'As
kingfishers catch fire' by Hopkins:

Each mortal thing does one thing and the same:
Deals out that being indoors each one dwells;
Selves – goes itself; *myself* it speaks and spells;
Crying *What I do is me: for that I came.*

I say more.

Now, an extract from Satire 5, by Donne:

> If all things be in all,
> As I think, since all, which were, are, and shall
> Be, be made of the same elements:
> Each thing, each thing implies or represents.
> Then man is a world.

This comparison will be found in a book by Thomas Docherty, *John Donne, Undone*. Hopkins and Donne are both discussing *haecceitas*, the quality of worldly objects. It is that quality that gives those objects their individuality as things. Hopkins is voicing a response theory, that everything exists in terms of the observer's consciousness. Donne sees every part of material creation as being a miniaturized reflection of the whole.

Yet the attempt to rationalize the physical reality of the world urges each poet into a similar mode of verse. This is the mode of verse Hopkins called sprung rhythm. Manifestly the rhythm was in use long before Hopkins's own time. The pattern is created not so much by the metrical feet as by the heavy stresses. Each poem is a set of five-stress lines. The rhythm is certainly *based* on an iambic pentameter, and to that extent the foot has relevance:

$$\breve{} \quad \acute{} \mid \breve{} \quad \acute{} \mid \breve{} \quad \acute{} \mid \acute{} \quad \breve{} \mid \breve{} \quad \acute{} \mid$$

Each mortal thing does one thing and the same . . . (Hopkins)

$$\breve{} \quad \acute{} \mid \breve{} \quad \acute{} \mid \breve{} \quad \acute{} \mid \breve{} \quad \acute{} \mid \breve{} \quad \acute{} \mid$$

Each thing, each thing implies or represents . . . (Donne)

But each and any foot may be reversed; that is to say, turned into an inversion. Further, there is a variable proportion of lightly stressed syllables to heavily stressed syllables. Though the ground-plan of the verse is metre, and that is described in terms of feet, the rhythm of a specific poem is best described in terms of heavier stresses (and pauses) in relation to lighter stresses. However, the number of light stresses is less important than the pattern of heavy stresses; that is to say, the relation of one stress to another.

What Donne and Hopkins and many other poets draw upon in their style and rhythm is 'the naked thew and sinew of the English language'. Those words belong to Hopkins's theory. Here is another example of Donne in practice. This is the beginning of his Satire 2, an attack upon poets and lawyers:

> Sir; though (I thank God for it) I do hate
> Perfectly all this town, yet there's one state
> In all ill things so excellently best,
> That hate, towards them, breeds pity towards the rest.
> Though poetry indeed be such a sin
> As I think that brings dearths, and Spaniards in,
> Though like the pestilence and old-fashioned love,
> Riddlingly it catch men; and doth remove
> Never, till it be starved out; yet their state
> Is poor, disarmed like papists, not worth hate.

One can see that the basis of this rocking, surging rhythm is the heroic couplet. But the metre is a launching-pad for the rhythm, and it is the rhythm that makes the poetry. There is a characteristic energy here, an eagerness of the voice. This is writing which becomes effective as speech. One feels compelled to speak such verse aloud:

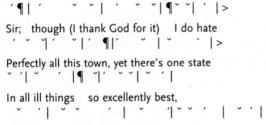

As was the case with Hopkins, a later poet felt the need to rewrite this piece by Donne as more formal metre. In this case, the later poet was Pope, and there is no doubt that his version has its virtues:

> Yes; thank my stars! as early as I knew
> This town, I had the sense to hate it too:
> Yet here, as ev'n in Hell, there must be still
> One giant-vice so excellently ill,
> That all beside one pities, not abhors;
> As who knows Sappho, smiles at other whores.
> I grant that poetry's a crying sin;
> It brought (no doubt) th'Excise and Army in:
> Catched like the plague, or love, the Lord knows how,
> But that the cure is starving, all allow.
> Yet like the Papist's is the Poet's state,
> Poor and disarmed, and hardly worth your hate.

Though Pope may have wanted to be strictly metrical here, there is in fact a pattern of pauses, as well as the occasional reversed foot, that livens up the rhythm:

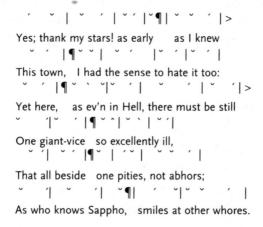

But it is not quite lively enough. Pope's metrical polish is achieved at some cost to the language. There are clichés that will not be found in the original: 'thank my stars!' and 'a crying sin'. There are phrases that look like makeweights: 'It brought (no doubt) th'Excise and Army in'. That 'no doubt' is padding, to bring the line up to its required five stresses.

Most palpable of all, there is an absence of individuality, of conviction. One would have one's doubts about this passage, even if ignorant of its provenance. It is a matter of the difference between Donne:

> Though like the pestilence and old-fashioned love,
> Riddlingly it catch men . . .

and Pope:

> Catched like the plague, or love, the Lord knows how . . .

Pope was capable of sprung rhythm, though never as variegated as that of Donne and Hopkins. It can occur as a special effect. It also occurs in his excursions into dialogue, which can be less decorous than his reputation as a 'correct' (that is to say, metrical) poet would lead one to suppose.

But Pope lived at a time of linguistically impoverished drama, while Donne frequented the theatres in the greatest period the English stage has ever had. When we hear the pattern of stresses in

> Though like the pestilence and old-fashioned love,
> Riddlingly it catch men . . .

we are hearing the non-theatrical counterpart to

> Though in the trade of war I have slain men,
> Yet do I hold it very stuff o' th' conscience
> To do no contrived murder.

That is from Shakespeare's *Othello*. Here, in terms of metric, we are much nearer to Hopkins's definition of sprung rhythm, and his

practice thereof, than either the theory or the practice of Sturge
Moore.

It is a matter of following the inflections of the voice without
losing the shape of the five-stress line. Often we find that
Shakespeare presses the rhythm far. Here, in *Cymbeline*, the excited
Imogen unseals a letter from her exiled husband:

> You good gods,
> Let what is here contained relish of love,
> Of my lord's health, of his content: yet not
> That we two are asunder – let that grieve him!
> Some griefs are med'cinable; that is one of them,
> For it doth physic love – of his content,
> All but in that. Good wax, thy leave. Blest be
> You bees that make these locks of counsel! Lovers
> And men in dangerous bonds pray not alike;
> Though forfeiters you cast in prison, yet
> You clasp young Cupid's tables. Good news, gods!

One way to define this as sprung rhythm is to indicate how
the verse departs from – without forgetting – a metric norm. The
metrical notation is the lower line above the verse; the rhythmic
notation the higher. They differ significantly:

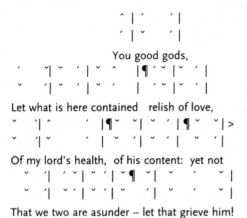

In the second line of the quotation just cited, the first foot, 'Let what', is, in rhythmic terms, an inversion, a trochee where one might expect an iamb. There is a distinct pause, that is to say more than a presumed caesura, after 'contained'. This has the effect of increasing the already heavy stress on the first syllable of 'relish'.

In the third line, the rhythmic notation of 'Of my lord's' is lighter than would be expected in strict metre. This has the effect of increasing the weight of stress on 'health' – which, after all, is the operative word here. A similar effect after 'health' is obtained by marking a pause. This not only adds to the weight of that word but lightens the stress on the next three syllables, 'of his con-', in order to stress more heavily the second syllable of 'content'.

There is a pause after 'content' which may be counted as part of the otherwise lightly stressed foot containing the words 'yet not'. These two light syllables, together with the enjambment that immediately follows, wing over the third line and on to the fourth line and the successive heavy stresses of 'we'/'two'. A rhythmic, as distinct from a metrical, reading suggests a quite distinct pause after 'asunder'. This makes for light syllables on 'let'/'that' which in their turn help to mark the heavy stress on 'grieve'.

The next line could be read as a hexameter. But it is more satisfactory to read this as a five-stress line with a number of light syllables:

    ˆ   ˘ |˘   ´ | ˘ ˘ ˘¶| `   ˘ |´   ˘   ˘ |
Some griefs are med'cinable; that is one of them . . .

The line begins with a medium stress, in order to keep it moving quickly. The first heavy stress, therefore, comes on the first syllable of 'med'cinable'. We can read the last three syllables of 'med'cinable' lightly, with a moderate pause afterwards. That pause prepares the way for two more light syllables on 'that is'. 'One', then, takes the key stress. The stress pattern shows how rhythm is related to meaning.

That word 'one', after all, is what is demonstrated or pointed at. Reading the line with a couple of light syllables after the final heavy stress causes that stress to stand out without sacrifice of the relative speed of the line. It suggests that this apparent hexameter, like many such, is really a pentameter with additional light syllables. It is worth remarking that even the most metrically conforming poets are liable to intersperse their five-stress lines with occasional hexameters, to secure emphasis. So it does not seem that a six-stress line exists in English as an entity on its own.

Shakespeare's sprung verse, then, substitutes stress pattern for regular feet. A rhythmic reading can be notated in terms of feet, as above, but they will include a number of what a metrical reading would hear as irregularities. Nevertheless, metrical conformity is not forgotten. There is a basic five-stress metre underlying the rhythm. That is what Hopkins called 'counterpointing'. Departure from metrical conformity does not obliterate metre. It survives as at once an echo and a point of reference. Such counterpointing, however, is by no means individual to Shakespeare.

It is true that the earlier Elizabethan drama tended to metrical conformity. But the successors of Shakespeare were, on the whole, more inclined to 'spring' their rhythm even than he was. *The Maid's Tragedy* by Francis Beaumont (1584–1616) and John Fletcher (1579–1625) in its time was thought the equal of Shakespeare's plays. Evadne, mistress of the king, is persuaded by her brother to murder the man who dishonoured her. Left alone, she laments her position:

> Oh, where have I been all this time? How friended,
> That I should lose myself thus desperately,
> And none for pity show me how I wandered?
> There is not in the compass of the light
> A more unhappy creature: sure I am monstrous;
> For I have done those follies, those mad mischiefs,
> Would dare a woman. O my loaden soul,

> Be not so cruel to me; choke not up
> The way to my repentance.

('Dare' means 'frighten'.) Any metrist could take out sundry light syllables and reduce this expressive rhythm to flat iambics:

> There is not in the compass of the light
> A more unhappy creature: I am monstrous.

There are more feminine endings than one would usually find in Shakespeare. These are endings on a light syllable: 'friended', 'desperately'. 'wandered', and so on. But they could be docked. One could amend 'how friended' to 'no friends', or 'desperately' to 'desperate'. The pararhyme 'friended' and 'wandered' could be deadened. But the amendment would mean that a good deal of the energy would depart. Exclamations such as 'Oh' and 'sure' are not padding, as so many of the lesser words in strict metre tend to be. They are the utterances of a weak and sensual creature on the brink of despair. One could try a revision:

> Oh, where have I been all this time? No friends,
> That I should lose myself thus desperate,
> And none for pity show me how I strayed?
> There is not in the compass of the light
> A more unhappy creature. I am weird
> For I have done those follies, those mad freaks,
> Would dare a woman . . .

But the text is better as Beaumont and Fletcher wrote it. Sprung rhythm is the life of verse drama, as it is of blank verse.

The same is true of other metres. The 'Skeltonics' of John Skelton were mentioned in the first chapter as examples of short lines. But short lines, especially the two-stress lines that Skelton favours, are liable to fall into monotony unless they are sprung, and this means that they are counterpointed. In 'Why come ye not to court' Skelton satirizes Henry VIII's chief minister, Cardinal Wolsey:

He ruleth all the roast
With bragging and with boast.
Borne up on every side
With pompë and with pride,
With 'Trump up, Alleluia!'
For dame Philargeria
Hath so his heart in hold
He loveth nothing but gold.

('Ruleth the roast' is a proverbial expression, meaning 'being in control'. 'Philargeria' means 'love of money'.)

This is a good deal more intricate than it may seem on the surface. The skipping rhythms are counterpointed by the metric notion of a dimeter, thus:

˘ ´ | ˘ ´ |
He ruleth all the roast . . .

But there is also the ghost of a three-stress line, a trimeter:

˘ ´|˘ ´| ˘ ´ |
He ruleth all the roast . . .

That particular ghost, however, is kept as a tenuous counterpoint by dint of the predominant tide of lines in which there are always two heavy stresses 'ruling the roast':

      ´   ´
Borne up on every side

      ´   ´
With pompë and with pride . . .

There can be medium-light and even medium stresses on such syllables as the first one of 'every', but they are the exception, and tend to merge with the plethora of lightly stressed syllables.

The metre, then, is a two-foot line, a dimeter. But the feet in which it is composed are subject to all kinds of wrenching, and there is certainly no rule as to light syllables:

˘ ´ | ˘˘ ˜ |
For dame Philargeria
˘ ˘ ˘ ´ | ˘ ´ |
Hath so his heart in hold
˘ ´ ˘ ˘ ˘ | ˘ ´ |
He loveth nothing but gold.

The tetrameter, too, is enlivened by being sprung. This is one of the oldest metres in English. It came over with the Normans and their French input into the basic Anglo-Saxon. Many romances from the thirteenth century onwards were written in tetrametric couplets.

Chaucer, in his earliest period, variegates the metre into sprung rhythm with accomplished ease. He translated much of a French allegorical poem which he called *The Romaunt of the Rose.* Here is a description of an old woman, who also represents Age itself:

Al woxen was her body unwelde,
And dry and dwined al for elde.
A foul, forwelked thing was she
That whilom round and soft had be.
Her ears shoken fast withal
As from her head they wolde fall;
Her face frounced and forpined,
And both her hondes lorn, fordwined.

('Unwelde' is 'unwieldy', in the sense of being feeble. 'Dwined' is 'dwindled', in the sense of being withered. 'Forwelked' is 'wrinkled'; 'forpined' is 'wasted away'; 'lorn' is 'lost'; and 'fordwined' is 'shrivelled up'.)

We shall not require detailed analysis to show how this verse transcends its metrical base. 'Al woxen was her body unwelde' has an extra syllable, 'un-', that gives the line a lilt. There is an enjambment which takes 'thing was she' over the line into 'That whilom'. One may choose to give 'ears' Chaucer's optional final *e* – 'eares'. But even so, the first syllable takes a weight of stress that contrasts with the subsequent 'shoken fast withal'. That part of the line is comparatively lightly stressed and should move quickly, to bring out the sense. The whole has an energetic effect, in contrast to the Old One's feebleness. It is as though the narrator were not lamenting the pathos of extreme old age so much as marvelling, almost rejoicing, at the spectacle of its physical oddity.

Without such devices of sprung rhythm, the tetrametric couplet would tend towards monotony. Every couple of generations it has renovated itself. The most striking change, however, came with the start of the nineteenth century. Presumably under the influence of the ballads, which will be discussed in Chapter 8, both Samuel Taylor Coleridge (1772–1834) and Sir Walter Scott (1771–1832) burst forth in tetrameters which their eighteenth-century predecessors would have found unorthodox. Here is an extract from a passage near the beginning of Coleridge's fragmentary narrative poem 'Christabel':

> Is the night chilly and dark?
> The night is chilly, but not dark.
> The thin gray cloud is spread on high,
> It covers but not hides the sky.
> The moon is behind, and at the full;
> And yet she looks both small and dull.
> The night is chill, the cloud is gray
> 'Tis a month before the month of May
> And the spring comes slowly up this way.

The iambic metre is not forgotten. But the inversions of individual feet cause the rhythm to dance along.

ˊ ˇ | ˊ ¶ | ˊ ˇ|ˇ   ˊ |

Is the night   chilly and dark?

This dancing effect is helped by the extra light syllables from time to time included.

ˇ   ˊ | ˇ ˇ ˊ | ˇ ˊ | ˇ ˊ |

The moon is behind, and at the full . . .

ˇ   ˇ   ˊ | ˇ   ˊ |ˇ ˊ | ˇ ˊ |

And the spring comes slowly up this way.

Sir Walter Scott took directly off from Coleridge. But his eight large-scale narrative poems are very far from being fragmentary, as Coleridge sometimes is. Scott employed tetrameters similar to those of 'Christabel' in *The Lay of the Last Minstrel*. Here is the beginning of Canto First:

> The feast was over in Branksome tower,
> And the Ladye had gone to her secret bower;
> Her bower that was guarded by word and by spell,
> Deadly to hear, and deadly to tell –
> Jesu Maria, shield us well!
> No living wight, save the Ladye alone,
> Had dared to cross the threshold stone.

These narratives of Scott were popular in their time, and the mode carried on through the nineteenth century. It has adapted less well to the twentieth. Here is John Masefield (1878–1967) chronicling a hunt from the quarry's point of view in *Reynard the Fox*:

> The fox was strong, he was full of running,
> He could run for an hour and then be cunning,
> But the cry behind him made him chill,
> They were nearer now and they meant to kill.

> They meant to run him until his blood
> Clogged on his heart as his brush with mud,
> Till his back bent up and his tongue hung flagging,
> And his belly and brush were filthed from dragging.

There is an absence of inner life in lines such as these. The energy is external. The enjambment from 'blood' to 'clogged' does not have much of an effect. If anything, it disperses the static idea of blood clogging. The internal rhyme in the penultimate line quoted, 'tongue'/'hung' has little effect. It seems to exist for its own sake. Further, the extra syllables employed do not acquire the lift and hurry that one finds in Coleridge, and even in Scott.

One cannot surmise how tetrameters could be employed in the later twentieth century except, perhaps, for broad satirical effects. The weight of narrative remains in sprung verse, but nowadays sprung verse functions best in the freer forms.

Francis Berry (b. 1915) has written sympathetically about Masefield. However, he employs his own rhythms in patterns that, if they owe something to Masefield, are more wide-ranging in their effects:

> The Sun, a slowing yellow Flange,
> Mellows palazzo, grange;
> The goatherd ducks from bat's sway flight;
> Shed lizard's tail curls up with sacred tinge,
> And Mediterranean stalls in evening light.

That is from a highly atmospheric poem, 'Mediterranean Year'. But it is a piece early in Berry's remarkable development. His main utilization of sprung verse, like that of many a modern narrative poet, is as a way of enhancing the exploratory rhythms of free verse. That is a matter that will be discussed in Chapter 7.

6

QUANTITY AND SYLLABICS

So far, rhythm in verse has been discussed as though it were a matter of stress. Another element that can be important, however, is quantity. Vowels, for example, can be of different length. There are both short and long vowels: a short *o* and a long *o*, for instance. The short *o* of 'loss' is made shorter by the fact that the word in which it occurs is stopped by a consonant at the end. This is usually what happens with respect to the short *o*: thus, 'boss', 'moss', 'toss'. The longer vowel of 'rose' is longer in itself because the long *o* seems to take more time to sound than the short *o* of 'loss'. This longer vowel need not necessarily be stopped by a consonant, but that consonantal stopping is one factor in 'rose' being shorter than 'woe'.

The vowel in the word 'loss' is short. The vowel in the word 'rose' is perceptibly longer. The vowel in the word 'woe' is the longest of the three. The respective lengths can be expressed in notation, thus:

    ˙   —   —

    loss   rose   woe

Length can be extended by the position in the line of verse of the syllable on which the word is placed. A word at the end of the line tends to acquire additional length:

—

Brought death into the world, and all our woe,
With loss of Eden.

It is also a question of syntax. The sentence does not finish with the end of the line. When the final word is heavily stressed, as here, this can leave it resonating, rather like a gong without an interceptor to make the resonance cease.

The words instanced will each be found in the first ten lines of Milton's *Paradise Lost*:

With loss of Eden . . .

—

Rose out of chaos . . .

—

. . . all our woe . . .

Milton has few rivals in the craft of manipulating quantity with respect to stress. For, great scholar of Greek and Latin that he was, he recognized that stress is the prime element in English rhythm, and that an English verse line is formed by its pattern of heavy stresses. Thus, quantity in Milton's hands is a way of counterpointing rhythm:

Brought death into the world, and all our woe . . .

The greater length in quantity of the vowel in 'woe' helps to secure a considerable extent of emphasis on that word when combined with other factors. 'Woe' carries a heavy stress and it is placed at the end of the line.

The craft that weights a line down can also lighten it. The Archfiend of Hell begins his eager journey to bring about the destruction of Mankind. Satan

```
 -    .    -    .    -    —  -    -  —    -   -
 `    ˘  |  ˘    ˆ  |  ˘   ˘   `  |  ˘  ˆ   |˘   ´  |
```

Puts on swift wings, and toward the gates of hell

```
 -    —    -   -   -  ⁻⁻ -   —
 ˘   ˆ   |  ˘   `  | ⌣˘  ´   |
```

Explores his solitary flight.

There are two heavy stresses: 'hell' and 'flight'. But the *e* of 'hell' is a short vowel, and the *i* of flight is a medium one – a potentially long syllable stopped by a consonant. This prevents the words in question, despite the heavy stresses placed upon them, taking their full possible emphasis. Thus, stress is played against quantity.

The longer vowels, such as the long *a* sound of 'gates' and the *or* sound of 'explores', do not occur on heavy stresses but on medium-heavy stresses. This, again, prevents the words in question being emphasized as much as is theoretically possible. Thus, quantity is played against stress. The effect is to keep the line – which is about flying swiftly – moving at a pace.

One of the fastest-moving passages in *Macbeth* is:

```
           ˆ   ˘|˘   `  | ˘  `  ˘  |
```
if th'assassination
```
 ˘       ˆ  |  ˘   `  |  ˘   `  |  ˘   `   |˘      `  | >
```
Could trammel up the consequence, and catch
```
 ˘     `  | ˘   ˆ   |  ˘   ˆ  |
```
With his surcease success.

There are no heavy stresses here. The medium stresses either occur on short vowels – 'if', 'tram-', '-cess' – or on a vowel that is prevented from being unduly long by dint of being stopped by a consonant – '-cease'. In this passage, pattern of stress and pattern of quantity are at one. Each serves to propel the line quickly.

With Wordsworth, the interplay between stress and quantity serves to bring about a hushed effect:

˘ ˆ | ˘ ˈ|˘ ˘ ˈ| ˘ ˈ| ˘ ˆ |>
A full half-hour together I have stood
ˊ ¶ | ˋ ˘ |˘ ˘ ˆ | ˘ ˋ | ˘ ˊ |

Mute,   looking at the grave in which he lies.

Here, the heavy stresses fall on words with longer vowels that are consonantally stopped: 'mute', 'lies'. Most of the stresses, however, are medium, and fall on the shorter vowels: 'full', 'stood', and on a consonantally stopped longer vowel, 'grave'. Of course, as with the action of syntax, the action of word association plays its part here. The subdued effect is aided not only by the avoidance of heavy stresses and the choice of shorter vowels but by the vocabulary: 'stood', 'mute', 'grave', 'lies'.

It should be understood from all this that quantity in English cannot function as an entity even to the extent that stress can. Quantity is very much dependent upon other elements. If we try to write verse with regard to quantity, seeking to ignore stress in the process, it tends to come out like this:

They wer'amid the shadows by night in loneliness obscure
Walking forth i'the void and vasty dominyon of Ades.

This is an attempt by Robert Bridges (1844–1930) to translate the sixth book of Virgil's *Aeneid*, using the Latin metre in which it was written. Latin metres are supposed to have been entirely quantitative, composed of long and short syllables, and deriving from ancient Greek.

It is hard, however, to imagine any rhythm without stress. Certainly, such readings as have been produced by such scholars as C. M. Bowra and K. J. Dover are remarkable for what would be recognized as rhythmic emphasis resembling that of English verse.

The Latin hexameter basically ran:

˜ ˘ | ˜ ˘ | ˜ ˘ | ˜ ˘ | ˜ ˘ | ´´|

where ´ represented a long syllable and ˘ represented a short syllable. There were variations, chiefly by way of substituting ´´ for ´ ˘ ˘ in any of the first five feet.

However it may have been in Latin, any attempt to reproduce this metre in English is going to run against the fact that quantity is a far more delicate element in the make-up of the rhythmic line than stress. There is, indeed, no way of avoiding stress's primacy. For all the distortions of language perpetrated by Bridges in an effort to achieve a quantitative hexameter, what he has here sounds like an awkward seven-stress line. Since no such line is stable in English, the effect is something like that of a four-stress alternating with a three-stress:

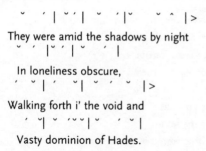

They were amid the shadows by night

In loneliness obscure,

Walking forth i' the void and

Vasty dominion of Hades.

This is ugly in its expression. Certainly, so far as one can judge such matters, it was not what Bridges intended. He was a good poet on his day; see his lyric describing evil in the world, 'Low Barometer'. But that fine poem is unmistakably written in rhythms based on stress patterns.

The theories of verse propounded by Robert Bridges were far removed from speech, unlike those of his friend Hopkins, and correspondingly academic. Yet he was right in surmising that the utilization of syllabics – quantitative verse in English – might reveal 'delicate and expressive rhythms hitherto unknown in our poetry'.

Bridges, however, was not the poet to bring this about. The attempt was made more imaginatively by his daughter, Elizabeth Daryush (1887–1977). She seems to have heard syllabics as a delicate tracery of sound counterpointing the normal stress pattern. Her form is to construct a line in terms of the syllables counted; rather than, that is to say, the stresses. For this to work, however, the stresses have to be held in check. It helps, too, if the subject is relatively subdued.

Daryush tends to be cautious in her approach, and stays close to the line of ten syllables. A good deal of her craft is expended in preventing this metre from falling into obvious blank verse. The approach seems to work in a poem called 'Still-Life'. Under the pretence of describing a perfect morning in the life of a favoured young mortal, Daryush succeeds in creating an atmosphere of *Ahnung*, full of brooding presentiment:

> Through the open French window the warm sun
> lights up the polished breakfast-table, laid
> round a bowl of crimson roses, for one –
> a service of Worcester porcelain, arrayed
> near it a melon, peaches, figs, small hot
> rolls in a napkin, fairy rack of toast,
> butter in ice, high silver coffee-pot,
> and, heaped on a salver, the morning's post.
>
> She comes over the lawn, the young heiress,
> from her early walk in her garden-wood
> feeling that life's a table set to bless
> her delicate desires with all that's good,
>
> that even the unopened future lies
> like a love-letter, full of sweet surprise.

One cannot help feeling that something very unpleasant indeed is waiting in the mail. It is partly the fact that the setting is all too

pretty. Partly, also, it is the reiterated image of communication –
'the morning's post', 'the unopened future'. But it is, as well, the
peculiar rhythm of Daryush's syllabics. She has shown a degree of
skill in avoiding the lure of iambic pentameters. If she does not
avoid stress patterns, at least she subdues them to the extent that
they counterpoint the quantitative measure of her vowels:

Through the open French window   the warm sun

lights up the polished breakfast-table, laid

round a bowl of crimson roses,   for one . . .

There is a sense of overrunning the line – not only a matter of
enjambment here – which is highly characteristic of syllabics. The
stress metre, which is inevitable however quantitatively the poet
hears her verse, is subverted. The foot-divisions do not tend to
coincide with the way in which the words themselves divide up as
separate entities:

| | | |

polished breakfast table crimson

Behind it all, the longer vowels are few, such as the *o* in 'open',
and when they occur they do not coincide with the heavier
stresses. But, then, heavier stresses also are few. When *they* occur,
they tend not to coincide with the longer vowels. 'Sun' and 'one' in
the poem are heavy stresses at the end of their respective lines, yet
their vowels are among the shorter ones.

This all makes for an underlying sense of uncertainty that effectively tinctures the ostensible optimism, even complacency, of the
poem. With a sure touch, Daryush has opened up a remarkable

area in twentieth-century poetry, curiously suited to an age of doubt. There were earlier attempts at syllabics – that is to say, counting syllables rather than hearing stresses – as far back as the Elizabethan period. But they do not sound at all like their counterparts in modern times.

Perhaps the poet most committed to this curious rhythm, and certainly its most remarkable practitioner, was Marianne Moore (1887–1972). Her superiority over Daryush can be located – though that is not the whole story – in her handling of rhyme. If there is a defect in 'Still-Life', it is that the poem still clings to tradition, to the tyranny of rhymes that are full: 'sun'/'one'; 'laid'/'arrayed'. This rather goes against the grain of syllabics, which is to be a chord rather than full harmony, an echo rather than counter-melody.

Moore, however, rhymes so discreetly that the unwary reader might take her exquisitely formal structures to be a kind of free verse. 'The Steeple-Jack' tells of a small town whose simple processes disguise the danger beneath the placid surface. It is an allegory of life. The reference with which the poem begins is to Albrecht Dürer (1471–1528), a German artist whose woodcuts included a visual representation of the Apocalypse, that book of the Bible which foretells the end of the world:

> Dürer would have seen a reason for living
>   in a town like this, with eight stranded whales
> to look at; with the sweet sea air coming into your house
> on a fine day, from water etched
>   with waves as formal as the scales
> on a fish.
>
> One by one, in two's, in three's, the seagulls keep
>   flying back and forth over the town clock,
> or sailing round the lighthouse without moving their wings –
> rising steadily with a slight

     quiver of the body – or flock
 mewing where

 a sea the purple of the peacock's neck is
     paled to greenish azure as Dürer changed
 the pine tree of the Tyrol to peacock blue and guinea
 grey. You can see a twenty-five-
     pound lobster and fish-nets arranged
 to dry. The

 whirlwind fife-and-drum of the storm bends the salt
     marsh grass, disturbs stars in the sky and the
 star on the steeple; it is a privilege to see so
 much confusion.

We hear more of that 'star on the steeple' later in the poem.

The quotation breaks off here because there is a breaking-off in the text. Moore in the original version of 'The Steeple-Jack' disrupted her stanza-form at this point, leaving a four-line stanza in discontinuity with the six-line stanza she had established. Later, she was to revise this poem, which is in her most recent *Collected Poems* a set of thirteen stanzas, each with six lines. What has happened is that two and a half lines have been added to complete the stanza, followed by five new stanzas, and then a half-line to start off the stanzas from the original draft that now complete this new version of the poem.

These new stanzas bring in a great deal of detail, relevant to the poem but not essential to it. The earlier version, then, is preferable. But there is no getting round the fact that the basic form in that original version has been broken as early as the fourth stanza.

The basic six-line stanza of the poem consists of lines whose syllable-count is as follows: 11, 10, 14, 8, 8, 3. This particular rhythm is probably as near quantitative verse as English will allow. There is also a subdued rhyme scheme, consisting mainly of blanks:

a b c d b e. The second and fifth lines of each of the regular stanzas recall one's attention, helped by the fact that they are indented, to the form beneath the apparently conversational utterance.

But you cannot get away from stress in English verse. There is, in addition to the syllabic count that determines the form, a more or less random pattern of stresses. They tend to the lighter end of the Trager–Smith scale, so as not to swamp the delicate play of the quantities:

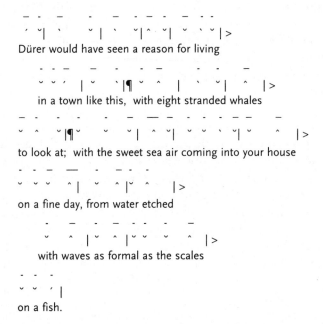

Notice that the quantities are predominantly medium and short. That corresponds to the stresses, which, as already indicated, are relatively unobtrusive, being mostly medium to light. The result is a line that would be spoken fairly rapidly and unemphatically.

This effect, as of talking in a relaxed fashion, is enhanced by what has already been pointed out as a characteristic of modern syllabics. That is the extensive degree of enjambment: 'living/in a'; 'whales/to look at'; 'house/on a fine day'; 'water etched/with'; 'as the scales/on a'. Every line in that stanza, except the last, flows over into the next. That is practically the case with each stanza in the poem.

The enjambment is not at all afraid to split up the syntax between lines. It will even sometimes leave the end of the line on an unimportant or unemphatic word: 'where'; 'is'; 'the'; 'so'; 'a'. When this happens, and the word in question is lightly stressed, it often has the effect of putting a stress on to the first syllable of the next line. This is also a noticeable characteristic of the first line, where there is no preliminary word to serve as enjambment. The word 'Dürer' acts as a propellant, to start the poem off with one of its relatively few heavy stresses.

The craft of Marianne Moore is preferable to that of Elizabeth Daryush. 'Still-Life' does not, as has been indicated, sufficiently safeguard itself against the careless reader. In an inadequate performance, the careful syllabics of Daryush could fall into a sort of iambic pentameter. This is unlikely to happen with Moore. The unlikelihood arises from the irregularity of Moore's stresses, together with the fact that they are, on the whole, lightly touched. As nearly as possible, they form a counterpoint with the quantities. It is a counterpoint in which the quantities are not altogether the junior partner.

Further, her exiguity of rhyme gives a sense of form without drawing too much attention to it. This is, given the exigencies of syllabics, preferable to the full rhyme of Daryush. We may infer from this that the creation of a rhythmic pattern by counting syllables is rather a restricted form of verse. But syllabics may be especially suited to certain kinds of meditative poetry, particularly that which dwells on the uncertainties of life. Moore ends her poem, ironically:

> It scarcely could be dangerous to be living
>   in a town like this, of simple people
> who have a steeple-jack placing danger-signs by the church

> when he is gilding the solid-
>   pointed star, which on a steeple
> stands for hope.

In a similar vein, Moore points out in 'To a Snail' the positive aspects of what might be seen as negative characteristics. This is really a poem about style, whose successes reside in economy, and in a reticence that does not render its means of achievement too explicit:

> If 'compression is the first grace of style',
> you have it. Contractility is a virtue
> as modesty is a virtue.
> It is not the acquisition of any one thing
> that is able to adorn,
> or the incidental quality that occurs
> as a concomitant of something well said,
> that we value in style,
> but the principle that is hid:
> in the absence of feet, 'a method of conclusions';
> 'a knowledge of principles',
> in the curious phenomenon of your occipital horn.

An 'occipital' horn is one that emerges from the *back* of the head – a reticent characteristic. The poem is both in concept and in rhythm based on an aphorism of the literary theorist known as 'Demetrius' (*c.* 50 BC), as translated from the Greek by Hamilton Fyfe: 'The very first grace of style is that which comes from compression.' It probably represents Moore's own view of her work. Consider the punning reference to the absence of feet. While one can certainly insert feet as a way of notating Moore's stress pattern, there can be no doubt that the feet are irregular. The prime method of ordering the verse is by stress. However, adjunctive to stress are the number of syllables per line, the pattern of quantity and also the rhyme scheme.

For example, here the shortest line (seven syllables) takes a heavy stress on its last syllable and is end-stopped; no enjambment. The line therefore acts as a kind of pivot in the poem. This is enhanced by the circumstance that the shortest line, line 5 of a twelve-line poem, carries the only rhyme. This line 5 accords with the final line, which is also the longest. But that accordance, though helping to shape the poem, does not call excessive attention to itself.

The interplay between stress and quantity gives the poem its peculiar tone, since the 'style' establishes itself through a number of factors that in other hands might turn out to be counter-productive. After all, it may not seem to be an advantage to live in a shell, as a snail does, but that could prove a protection against being amorphous.

Marianne Moore has, in her quiet way, been influential upon a number of younger poets. Thom Gunn (b. 1929) has no very settled personality or style in his writing but is adept at realizing the traits of other poets. He is not a snail, perhaps, so much as a hermit crab. It is the snail, however, that he considers in what is at once an imitation of Moore and a convincing demonstration of syllabics at play. 'Considering the Snail':

> The snail pushes through a green
> night, for the grass is heavy
> with water and meets over
> the bright path he makes, where rain
> has darkened the earth's dark. He
> moves in a wood of desire,
> pale antlers barely stirring
> as he hunts. I cannot tell
> what power is at work, drenched there
> with purpose, knowing nothing.
> What is a snail's fury? All
> I think is that if later

> I parted the blades above
> the tunnel and saw the thin
> trail of broken white across
> litter, I would never have
> imagined the slow passion
> to that deliberate progress.

The suppressed fact is that the snail has the characteristics of both genders. Though suppressed as regards explicit utterance, this ability to switch sexual roles is a factor in the poem. Further: although the snail may seem slow-moving, it is intent on activity. After all, it succeeds in propagating itself. Indeed, the snail is a successful animal.

Such phrases as 'a wood of desire', 'drenched there/with purpose' and 'slow passion' suggest that the purpose of the snail's deliberate progress is copulation. The pale antlers – another emblem of this slow chase – are 'barely stirring'. That 'barely' refers at once to the vulnerable quality of the snail's horns and to their almost undetectable movement. Again, this last quality – undetectable movement – is what attaches itself to the whole motion of the snail. That is why the rhythm of syllabics is appropriate here.

Each line contains seven syllables. As is the case with Moore, the line-endings are blurred by enjambment. There is no hesitation about breaking the syntactic flow. There is none, either, about ending the line on unimportant words. All this serves to enhance the faint music of the quantities. This music, as has been said, echoes the stealthy but determined movement of the snail.

The attempt to measure the line by quantity is especially effective with poems that are elliptical in subject. This is particularly the case in the work of George MacBeth, a poem of whose was discussed in Chapter 2. Though blank verse is often his chosen medium, he is equally at home in syllabics. His poem 'The Killing' is a comment on Milton's line 'brought death into the world'. It narrates a group of men taking out to sea a poisoned ash with the capability of destroying the world. This appears to be an attempt at disposal that goes disastrously wrong. The reader, however, is only gradually let into the secret:

> In a wooden room, surrounded by lights and
>   Faces, the place where death had
> Come to its sharpest point was exposed. In a
>   Clear shell they examined the
>   Needle of death. How many
> Million deaths were concentrated in
>
> A single centre! The compass of death was
>   Lifted, detached and broken,
> Taken and burned. The seed of death lay in the
>   Hold. Without disturbance or
>   Ceremony they sealed it
> In foil. The ship stirred at the quay. The
>
> Pilot was ready. A long shadow slanted
>   On the harbour water. The
> Fin bearing the ignorant crew on their brief
>   Journey cut through the air. Three
>   Furlongs out at sea the
> Strike of the engine fell. The screws turned . . .

The syllabic count of the lines in each six-line stanza is as follows: 11, 7, 11, 7, 7, 9. There is no rhyming. The subjugation of stress in favour of quantity is partly brought about by the short sentences, the extent of enjambment, and the way in which that enjambment overruns syntactical patterning. No stanza is self-contained. The first stanza has no syntactical end, hardly even pausing at 'concentrated in'. In the last stanza quoted, the screws turn on, into the next stanza.

The syllabic rhythm here has a quiet insistence; almost a nagging quality. It is redeemed from monotony by the way in

which the author plays the syllabic pattern against the stress
pattern:

```
 .   .   .     .   .   _      .   _   .   _  _    .
 ˇ   ˇ   ´     ˇ   ˇ   |¶  ˇ  ˇ     ˇ   ˇ  ´      ˇ  | >
In a wooden room,  surrounded by lights and

     _   .   .   .   .
     ´  ˇ |¶  ˇ   ˇ      ˇ      ´        ˇ | >
   Faces,  the place where death had

 .      _  .    _   .     _      .   .    _    .  .
 ´     ˇ ˇ |  ´   ˇ |  ´     ˇ  ˇ |  ´    ˇ  ˇ | >
   Come to its sharpest point was exposed. In a . . .
```

Notice there are few syllables that one could call really long. When
there is a long vowel, it is usually subordinated by being given to
an unimportant word placed on a lightly stressed syllable, such as
'by'. Similarly, one finds on heavily stressed syllables such short
vowels as those in 'wood(en)', 'death', 'come'. This latter effect is
not universal, but it is certainly noticeable. Such words as these,
falling on heavy stresses, are, though short in quantity, important
in syntax and meaning. So one gets an effect of counterpoint: one
mode of rhythm played against another; quantity against stress.
This adds to the complexity, and consequently to the extent of
attention one has to give the poem when reading it aloud.

If the quantity of the vowels went along with the stresses and the
meanings, we would have something almost approaching a succes-
sion of dactylic feet: ´ ˇ ˇ | ´ ˇ ˇ | ´ ˇ ˇ |. One hears the tendency in
such a phrase as '(sur)rounded by lights and/Faces'. But dactyls
would prove too decisive for this particular theme.

The metre, therefore, is prevented from becoming simply
dactylic by the methods the poet adopts to keep quantity to the
forefront, and it is most certainly not a pattern of quantity that
lends itself to any dactylic pattern. The vowels are too short and
the syntax too broken to permit any such rhythm to take over.
Therefore this form of syllabics, almost certainly learned from

Moore, is appropriate to the unheroic subject of death entering the world, like a science with good intentions, and finishing it off altogether.

The subdued, the elliptic, the quietly insistent – all these are tones best conveyed in syllabics. The rhythm has to the more usual modes of writing something of the relation of the precursors of the piano to the resonant modern instrument.

Because of this, it may seem relevant for the present author to end this chapter with a poem in lines of seven syllables each that he wrote concerned with one such predecessor: the clavichord. This is a small keyboard instrument, with metal tangents that push against rather than strike the strings. It may seem limited, as indeed syllabics may, but some master musicians wrote for it.

The clavichord is uniquely suitable for performing at home rather than on a platform. In that regard, it resembles poetry itself. Here is 'The Clavichord Speaks':

> When you feel rather than hear
> Music, that is my voice. No
> Wresting of your heart's strings but
> Chords sounding in sympathy.
>
> Come then, poor time-torn man, leave
> The crowded traffic of the
> Pestering city, and sit
> Down at my keys, open your
>
> Sad heart – I, the Clavichord,
> Speak to you. Bach knew how these
> Small sounds, near-inanition,
> Expressed, not gestured, called for
>
> No virtuoso, needed
> No hall or audience, but
> Just one's wife, a friend perhaps,
> One's room, sector in chaos,

Or just an ear, your own. So
Poetry emerges out of
The quiet voice, until you
Sense no barrier between

You and the verse – voice subsumed
In content. And this voice here
Does not play Bach but is Bach
Himself speaking not to you

But within you, sounding the
Chords common to both, to all
Men, so rarely touched these swift
Days when only the shout is

Heard, impinging on the thick-
ened sense, roar of the city.
Days when only the rude shove
Tells, all grace and kindness spent.

Sad that I, an antique, so
Long survive my time, as the
Voice of the past masters not
Yet wholly discredited

Survives in my strings alone,
Elsewhere coarsened past knowledge,
Beyond belief. So sit then,
Friend, rest on these keys, only

Here to find recompense for
Your labours, only here to
Find men that were men, barriers
Melted away, speak to you.

7

FREE VERSE

Free verse should not be thought of as a kind of verse without form. On the contrary, there are three quite distinct varieties of writing which shelter under this blanket denomination. Each variety has quite enough form to make it distinct from the other, and from any other kind of verse.

Not one of those three varieties, however, answers to the following description, circulated by several scholars and put forward authoritatively by Paull F. Baum in his book *The Principles of English Versification*. Baum says that some kinds of free verse 'do not aim to be more than ordinary prose printed in segments more or less closely corresponding with the phrase rhythm or normal sound rhythms of language'. Such writing as this – and one must agree with Baum that there has been a good deal of it in the twentieth century – is not verse of any sort, free or otherwise.

Amateur poets are especially prone to this kind of writing. A recent example, part of a competition which the present author helped to judge, ran thus:

I know of a game
played by many

> without definite
> rules – that is
> hopelessly
> [mis]understood.
>
> a game at which
> I do not wish
> to win or lose
> only continue
> to [un]earth
> more complex tactics
> and engaging moves.

This appears to be a disquisition on poetry, though it may also be treating poetry as a metaphor for love. What it cannot be called is verse. There is little difference if we write it out as prose:

> I know of a game played by many without definite rules, that is hopelessly [mis]understood. A game at which I do not wish to win or lose, only continue to [un]earth more complex tactics and engaging moves.

If anything, the piece is improved by being set out as prose, together with some rectifying of the punctuation. In that form, it seems to be a kind of resolution to improve craftsmanship in whatever art the author is contemplating, rather than to be competitive against other people. The sentiment is admirable. The expression, too, has its virtues. But those virtues are not rhythmic ones.

This is a well-meant amateur contribution to a competition. But the most distinguished poets can fall into velleity when attempting free verse. The desire is there, but not the performance. For example, the Poet Laureate, Ted Hughes (b. 1930), is the author of masterpieces such as 'The Martyrdom of Bishop Farrar', 'Six Young Men', 'Wind' and 'Relic'. He is also the author of 'Revenge Fable', published as part of his sequence *Crow*:

> There was a person
> Could not get rid of his mother
> As if he were her topmost twig.
> So he pounded and hacked at her
> With numbers and equations and laws
> Which he invented and called truth.
> He investigated, incriminated
> and penalized her, like Tolstoy,
> Forbidding, screaming and condemning,
> Going for her with a knife,
> Obliterating her with disgusts
> Bulldozers and detergents
> Requisitions and central heating
> Rifles and whisky and bored sleep.
> With all her babes in her arms, in ghostly weepings,
> She died.
> His head fell off like a leaf.

There is a vestigial form here, but it has little to do with verse. Rather, certain connections are established through a sequence of past participles – 'investigated . . . incriminated . . . penalized . . . ' – and present participles: 'Forbidding . . . screaming . . . condemning . . . .'.

Otherwise, there is little to determine where one line ends and another begins. One could, for instance, read the opening lines as:

> There was a person could not get rid of his mother
> As if he were her topmost twig. So he
> Pounded and hacked at her with numbers and equations
> And laws which he invented and called truth.

This recension is no more satisfactory as verse than the original. We cannot determine an extent of precedence for the one over the other.

Further: the poem does not work as a rhythmic unit. You could take out, say, lines 7–9, so that the poem goes from 'Which he invented and called truth' to 'Going for her with a knife'. The omitted lines would not create a hiatus. Rhythmically, as well as argumentatively, the poem would be unimpaired by their absence. You could, alternatively, take out lines 11–14. The poem would then go from 'Going for her with a knife' to 'With all her babes in her arms, in ghostly weepings'. Very little would be lost in such a lesion. Indeed, by avoiding an incidence of melodrama, the poem could be held to have been improved.

It is therefore possible for so distinguished a poet as Hughes to attempt a poem in free verse that comes out as chopped-up prose. This suggests that free verse is a difficult form in which to write. The variety that has proved most successful is debatably not free verse at all. A more logical name for it is free blank verse. To give any idea of how this, the most widespread form of free verse, came about, some account must be given of the development of its parent form, blank verse itself.

Blank verse, as has already been indicated, emerged in the mid-sixteenth century as an invention by the Earl of Surrey. Subsequently, it was used mostly for drama.

The first play to be written in blank verse was *Gorboduc* by Thomas Sackville (1536–1608) and Thomas Norton (1532–84). It exhibits traits similar to those of Surrey's translation of the *Aeneid*, in that its verse resolutely conforms to metre and admits little variety of rhythm. In a feeble anticipation of *King Lear*, an aged king is advised about his sons:

> If flattery then, which fails not to assail
> The tender minds of yet unskilful youth,
> In one shall kindle and increase disdain,
> And envy in the other's heart inflame,
> This fire shall waste their love, their lives, their land,
> And ruthful ruin shall destroy them both.

But, as the drama developed, blank verse became more varied and therefore more capable of poetry. The first practitioner of dramatic blank verse whose work can be performed effectively today was Christopher Marlowe (1564–93). His *Tamburlaine the Great* seems metrically formal, compared with later developments, but it still manages to incorporate a characteristic lyrical swing. Speaking of poets and their limitations, Tamburlaine says:

> If these had made one poem's period,
> And all combined in beauty's worthiness,
> Yet should there hover in their restless heads
> One thought, one grace, one wonder, at the least,
> Which into words no virtue can digest.

There is a degree of emphasis here new to English poetry in that metrical form. The novelty may be located in the variety of stress; for example:

> ´   ˇ | ˇ   ´|ˇ¶|ˇ   ˇ   ^ |ˇ   ´ |
> Yet should there hover   in their restless heads . . .

Here is an inverted first foot, together with some lightly stressed syllables in the middle – more lightly stressed than would be the norm with a strictly metrical line of blank verse. In that inheres the lyrical swing.

Shakespeare was slow to learn from this more precocious contemporary. His earlier verse, in *Richard III* for example, seems end-stopped and attached to metre. Richard gives his attraction to Lady Anne as his reason for killing Edward, Prince of Wales, her husband:

> Your beauty was the cause of that effect –
> Your beauty that did haunt me in my sleep
> To undertake the death of all the world
> So I might live one hour in your sweet bosom.

Shakespeare's personal development was in some respects

similar to that of the Elizabethan and Jacobean drama at large. His middle period finds him using a more flexible line. There are fewer feet conforming to iambics, and more use of enjambment.

In *Troilus and Cressida*, Ulysses warns Achilles about turns of fashion:

> Time hath, my lord, a wallet at his back
> Wherein he puts alms for oblivion,
> A great-sized monster of ingratitudes.
> Those scraps are good deeds past, which are devoured
> As fast as they are made, forgot as soon
> As done . . .

This has a variety of stress exceeding that found in Marlowe. One finds a not dissimilar freedom in a play of the same period, *The Revenger's Tragedy*, usually thought to be by Cyril Tourneur (?1575–1626), though claims have been recently made for a very different dramatist, Thomas Middleton (1580–1627). Here, in terms that have been developed from both Tamburlaine and Richard III, Spurio describes the presumed occasion of his bastardy:

> In such a whispering and withdrawing hour,
> When base male-bawds kept sentinel at stair-head,
> Was I stolen softly. O damnation meet!
> The sin of feasts, drunken adultery!

As the seventeenth century matured, dramatic verse grew even freer; with apparently incomplete lines, increased enjambment and a recognizable degree of sprung rhythm. An example produced ten years after Shakespeare's death is *The Roman Actor* by Philip Massinger (1583–1640). The senators are deploring the decadence of Rome under the theatre-loving emperor, Domitian:

> So dangerous the age is, and such bad acts
> Are practised everywhere, we hardly sleep,

> Nay, cannot dream with safety. All our actions
> Are called in question; to be nobly born
> Is now a crime; and to deserve too well,
> Held capital treason . . .

What these excerpts from *Troilus and Cressida*, *The Revenger's Tragedy* and *The Roman Actor* have in common is not so much a rhythmic likeness as a rhythmic *un*likeness to the metrical norm or blueprint. In this respect, these plays look forward to later developments. Consider each respective first line:

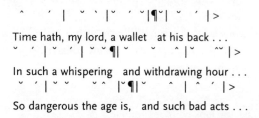

Time hath, my lord, a wallet   at his back . . .

In such a whispering   and withdrawing hour . . .

So dangerous the age is,   and such bad acts . . .

T. S. Eliot (1888–1965) is often thought to be the supreme master of free verse. But this American took his tune from these Jacobean poetic dramatists, and what he writes is a free *blank* verse. Here is an anti-hero, Gerontion, excusing his lack of action:

> After such knowledge, what forgiveness? Think now
> History has many cunning passages, contrived corridors
> And issues, deceives with whispering ambitions,
> Guides us by vanities. Think now
> She gives when our attention is distracted
> And what she gives, gives with such supple confusions
> That the giving famishes the craving. Gives too late
> What's not believed in, or if still believed,
> In memory only, reconsidered passion. Gives too soon
> Into weak hands, what's thought can be dispensed with
> Till the refusal propagates a fear.

Whatever one can say about added syllables, enjambment and sprung verse generally, there is a definite five-stress rhythm going through all of this:

and so on. Sometimes Eliot is nearer to his exemplars even than this.

In a play, *The Changeling*, which Middleton wrote with William Rowley (?1585–?1625), there is a sullied heroine, Beatrice-Joanna, confessing her fault to her father:

> I am that of your blood was taken from you
> For your better health; look no more upon it,
> But cast it to the ground regardlessly,
> Let the common sewer take it from distinction.
> Beneath the stars, upon yon meteor,
> Ever hung my fate, 'mongst things corruptible;
> I ne'er could pluck it from him; my loathing
> Was prophet to the rest, but ne'er believed;
> Mine honour fell with him, and now my life.

(The 'meteor' is her lover, De Flores.) This, though with its five-stress basis recognizably blank verse, is noticeably free. Eliot, owing nothing conceptually to the passage, nevertheless takes up its rhythm with considerable urgency in 'Gerontion':

> I that was near your heart was removed therefrom
> To lose beauty in terror, terror in inquisition.
> I have lost my passion: why should I need to keep it
> Since what is kept must be adulterated?

I have lost my sight, smell, hearing, taste and touch:
How should I use them for your closer contact?

This, though noticeably free, has a five-stress basis and is recognizably blank verse. Eliot has matched the associative habit, which is a characteristic of American poetry, to the rhythms of the Jacobean drama. This is an extraordinary thing to have done if we reflect that the drama depends on defined plot and is in other ways different from Eliot's craft of impressionistic monologue. It is a remarkable act of adaptation that picks out those qualities of texts three hundred years after their time that best suit the conditions of the twentieth century.

In his most famous poem, *The Waste Land*, Eliot described his century in terms of sexual malaise. To describe a mismated couple he drew upon one of Shakespeare's later plays, *Antony and Cleopatra*:

The barge she sat in like a burnished throne
Burned on the water: the poop was beaten gold;
Purple the sails, and so perfumed that
The winds were love-sick with them.

Eliot's fine lady is a kind of caricature of Cleopatra, and her domestic setting imitates Egyptian splendour with inappropriate extravagance:

The Chair she sat in, like a burnished throne,
Glowed on the marble, where the glass
Held up by standards wrought with fruited vines
From which a golden Cupidon peeped out . . .

As the scene proceeds, it is not so much Shakespeare that is drawn upon as John Webster (?1578–?1632), a figure very important to Eliot. First, we find a link with his play *The Devil's Law-Case*, when Eliot turns an Elizabethan idiom into a modern atmospheric detail:

'Did he not groan?'
>
> 'Is the wind in that door still?'

Eliot picks this up and renders it as an item in the couple's quarrel.

'What is that noise?'
>
> The wind under the door.

Then Webster's *The White Devil* is brought into service for the next few lines:

> 'What dost think on?'
>
'Nothing; of nothing: leave thy idle questions.
I am i'the way to study a long silence:
To prate were idle. I remember nothing.'

Eliot adapts this to:

'What is that noise now? What is the wind doing?'
>
> Nothing again nothing.
>
> > 'Do
>
You know nothing? Do you see nothing? Do you remember
Nothing?'

It was perhaps from Webster that Eliot learned most of his versification. The influence is prevalent. Webster's *The White Devil* has:

> they'll remarry
Ere the worm pierce your winding-sheet, ere the spider
Make a thin curtain for your epitaphs.

Towards the end of *The Waste Land* this comes out as:

By this, and this only, we have existed
Which is not to be found in our obituaries
Or in memories draped by the beneficent spider
Or under seals broken by the lean solicitor.

It is not only a matter of verbal resemblance, but also, what almost always goes along with that, a marked affinity in rhythm. What appears often to be, in Webster, a loose and sometimes broken-backed blank verse is, with surprisingly little alteration, transformed by Eliot into his own brand of free verse.

Of course, this was not the only rhythm Eliot subscribed to, although it is probably the one for which he is best known. One may also remark that the Jacobean influence thinned out rather as his work went on. Yet in Eliot's last important poem, a work of 1942 called 'Little Gidding', the Jacobean rhythm still has its echoes. One may hear, at the beginning, the movement of a speech from *The Lover's Melancholy* by John Ford (1586–?1639):

> Minutes are numbered by the fall of sands,
> As by an hourglass; the span of time
> Doth waste us to our graves, and we look on it:
> An age of pleasures, revelled out, comes home
> At last, and ends in sorrow; but the life,
> Weary of riot, numbers every sand,
> Wailing in sighs, until the last drop down;
> So to conclude calamity in rest.

Eliot had commended this speech from a not very satisfactory play as far back as 1932, when his essay on Ford was published, and here Ford's melancholy but insistent rhythm still lingers:

> Midwinter spring is its own season
> Sempiternal though sodden towards sundown,
> Suspended in time, between pole and tropic.
> When the short day is brightest, with frost and fire,
> The brief sun flames the ice, on pond and ditches,
> In windless cold that is the heart's heat,
> Reflecting in a watery mirror
> A glare that is blindness in the early afternoon.

Additionally, a couple of pages further on, in a passage renowned for qualities resembling those of the Italian poet Dante (1265–1321), Eliot picks up intonations from the much less exalted poet Tourneur, found in his play *The Atheist's Tragedy*:

It could no longer endure to see the man
Whom it had slain, yet loath to leave him, with
A kind of unresolved unwilling pace.

That uneasy leave-taking, the sea departing from the man thought drowned, is found at the end of a dialogue between Eliot and a mysterious elder poet:

The day was breaking. In the disfigured street
He left me with a kind of valediction,
And faded on the blowing of the horn.

What should be clear by now is that the free verse with which Eliot is credited can more accurately be characterized as free blank verse. Many poets have imitated Eliot in this: Herbert Read (1893–1968), Edwin Muir (1887–1959), Allen Tate (1899–1979), Hart Crane (1899–1932), and, of course, W. H. Auden. One can only suppose that they were aware of following the Elizabethans and Jacobeans at one remove – those Elizabethans and Jacobeans about whom, as a critic, Eliot had written so eloquently.

The mode of Eliot, as has already been indicated, is only one variety of free verse. Apart from a tendency to draw upon prose sources, especially at the beginning of poems, it has little in common with another variety of free verse, one associated with Walt Whitman (1819–92). That is more properly called cadenced verse. Like free blank verse, it has clear antecedents. Most of all, it would seem to derive from the Authorized Version of the Bible.

The Bible is, by convention, written out as prose. But a good many chapters have the emphasis and lyricism of poetry. It is true that there is no such thing as a tight stanza form, or even a rhyme scheme. An attentive ear, however, will perceive a recognizable pattern of strophe. That is to say, there is a tendency for the language to form itself into groups of lines that resemble the disposition of a lyric poem.

The Song of Solomon is one such example. Theologically, it has been regarded as an expression of Christ's love for his Church. To the lay reader, it is likely to come across as an uninhibitedly erotic poem, vigorously addressing a young woman:

> Behold thou art fair, my love; behold, thou art fair; thou hast doves' eyes within thy locks: thy hair is as a flock of goats, that appear from mount Gilead.
>
> Thy teeth are like a flock of sheep that are even shorn, which came up from the washing; whereof every one bear twins, and none is barren among them.
>
> Thy lips are like a thread of scarlet, and thy speech is comely: thy temples are like a piece of pomegranate within thy locks.
>
> Thy neck is like the tower of David builded for an armoury, whereon there hang a thousand bucklers, all shields of mighty men.
>
> Thy two breasts are like two young roes that are twins, which feed among the lilies.
>
> Until the day break, and the shadows flee away, I will get me to the mountain of myrrh, and to the hill of frankincense.
>
> Thou art all fair, my love, there is no spot in thee.
>
> Come with me from Lebanon, my spouse, with me from Lebanon: look from the top of Amana, from the top of Shenir and Hermon, from the lions' dens, from the mountains of the leopards.
>
> Thou hast ravished my heart, my sister, my spouse; thou hast ravished my heart with one of thine eyes, with one chain of thy neck.
>
> How fair is thy love, my sister, my spouse! how much better is thy love than wine! and the smell of thine ointment than all spices!

> Thy lips, O my spouse, drop as the honeycomb: honey and milk are under thy tongue; and the smell of thy garments is like the smell of Lebanon.
>
> A garden inclosed is my sister, my spouse; a spring shut up, a fountain sealed.
>
> Thy plants are an orchard of pomegranates, with pleasant fruits; camphire, with spikenard,
>
> Spikenard and saffron; calamus and cinnamon, with all trees of frankincense; myrrh and aloes, with all the chief spices;
>
> A fountain of gardens, a well of living waters, and streams from Lebanon.
>
> Awake, O north wind; and come, thou south; blow upon my garden, that the spices thereof may flow out.

There are several devices that link the disparate phrases in this rhapsody and make it cohere as a poem. First, there is the repetition of certain key words, such as 'Lebanon', and of phrases such as 'my sister, my spouse'. Then there is catalogue: 'thy teeth . . . thy neck . . . thy two breasts'. Further, there is parallelism, whereby one phrase is made to counterbalance another which closely resembles it: 'Thy lips, O my spouse, drop as the honeycomb: honey and milk are under thy tongue'. There is, also, a good deal of internal rhyme and pararhyme: 'locks'/'flock'; 'Lebanon'/ 'Hermon'; 'south'/'out'. Still further, there is a patterning of alliteration: 'sheep'/'shorn'; 'bear'/'barren'.

The most salient aspect, however, is the rhythm. The point can best be made by writing out some of this apparent prose as verse:

> Behold, thou art fair, my love; behold thou art fair;
> Thou hast doves' eyes within thy locks: thy hair is as a flock of
>   goats, that appear from mount Gilead.
> Thy teeth are like a flock of sheep that are even shorn, which came
>   up from the washing;
> Whereof every one bear twins, and none is barren among them.

> Thy lips are like a thread of scarlet, and thy speech is comely:
> Thy temples are like a piece of pomegranate within thy locks.

Laid out in this manner, the lines seem like loose hexameters. They comprise six heavy or medium stresses, and any number of light or even unaccented syllables. The metrical ideas of Gerard Manley Hopkins are fulfilled in cadenced verse and prose more than in any other form. Here we have not only a varying number of light stresses, but also the outrides, those syllables which may be held to take no stress. In addition, there is an effect by which one line seems to be set against another. The sign » will be used to signify the line which, so to speak, thrusts. The sign « will be used to signify the line which receives the thrust:

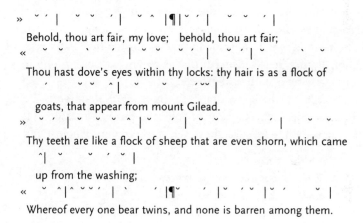

The tendency is for the lighter syllables to go especially rapidly in this particular variety of loose line. It has been previously remarked that the hexameter in English is unstable. This instability is here put to good use, since it means there can be long lines of variable content without losing a sense of form. The rapid patter of light syllables and outrides balances the six (sometimes it is five) stresses that determine the line:

» ˘ ′ | ˘ ˘ ˘ ′ | ˘ ′ ˘|¶˘ | ˘ ′ | ˘ ′ ˘|

Thy lips are like a thread of scarlet, and thy speech is comely:

« ˘ ′ ˘| ˘ ˘ ˘ ^ | ˘ ′ ′| ˘ ˘ ¶| ˘ ^ | ˘ ′ |

Thy temples are like a piece of pomegranate within thy locks.

The poet who learned most, most creatively, from the cadences of the Bible was, as has already been said, Whitman. Yet this American's verse was assailed on first publication for being aggressively modern. Indeed, those sections of it that most resembled the Song of Solomon were declared to be obscene. It only goes to show how far critics could lose their sense of tradition. They had forgotten their Bible.

The resemblance between the Song of Solomon and Whitman is not only one of erotic ardour. It is not only a matter of vocabulary, either, though vocabulary always goes along with rhythm. The verse in which Whitman wrote is not the free blank verse of Eliot. Rather, it is cadenced; that is to say, written in long loose lines deriving from lyrical prose.

One poem which owes most to the Song of Solomon is 'I Sing the Body Electric'. The Song of Solomon treats of a season of love; 'I Sing the Body Electric', however, celebrates one single night:

> This is the female form,
> A divine nimbus exhales from it from head to foot,
> It attracts with fierce undeniable attraction,
> I am drawn by its breath as if I were no more than a helpless vapor . . .
>   all falls aside but myself and it,
> Books, art, religion, time . . . the visible and solid earth . . . the
>   atmosphere and the fringed clouds . . . what was expected of
>   heaven or feared of hell are now consumed,
> Mad filaments, ungovernable shoots play out of it . . . the response
>   likewise ungovernable,
> Hair, bosom, hips, bend of legs, negligent falling hands – all
>   diffused . . . mine too diffused,

Ebb stung by the flow and flow stung by the ebb . . . loveflesh
   swelling and deliciously aching,
Limitless limpid jets of love hot and enormous . . . quivering jelly of
   love . . . white-blow and delirious juice,
Bridegroom-night of love working surely and softly into the prostrate
   dawn,
Undulating into the willing and yielding day,
Lost in the cleave of the clasping and sweetfleshed day.

This is the nucleus . . . after the child is born of woman, the man is
   born of woman,
This is the bath of birth . . . this is the merge of small and large and
   the outlet again.

Be not ashamed women . . . your privilege encloses the rest . . . it is
   the exit of the rest,
You are the gates of the body and you are the gates of the soul.

The female contains all qualities and tempers them . . . she is in her
   place . . . she moves with perfect balance,
She is all things duly veiled . . . she is both passive and active . . .
   she is to conceive daughters as well as sons and sons as well as
   daughters.

As I see my soul reflected in nature . . . as I see through a mist one
   with inexpressible completeness and beauty . . . see the bent head
   and arms folded over the breast . . . the female I see.

The convention is that each line should be deemed of equal
length. This means that the shorter lines are more heavily stressed.
The longer lines, therefore, have more lightly stressed syllables
and carry more outrides. These lightly stressed syllables and,
still more, the outrides, are consequently taken at a considerable
pace.

In this particular instance, the three opening lines are heavy, almost portentous, weighted down not only by stress but by pause:

»   ′¶ ′¶ ˘ ′| ^ ¶| ′   ¶|¶

  This is the female form,

«˘ ˘ ′ |¶ ′   ˘|¶|˘ ′ | ˘ ˘¶|˘   ′ | ˘ ′ |

  A divine nimbus exhales from it from head to foot,

»˘ ˘ ′ |¶| ˘   ˜ |¶′| ˘ ′|˘ ˘¶|˘   ′   ˘ |

  It attracts   with fierce undeniable   attraction,

«˘˘   `    ˘  ˘   ′  |  ˘ ˘ ˘  `   ˘   ′   ˘| ˘ ′   ˘ | ′ ˘ ¶|

  I am drawn by its breath as if I were no more than a helpless vapor . . .

     `   `   ˘ ′   ˘| `  ` ˘   ′|

    all falls aside but myself and it . . .

The fourth line, by contrast to the first three, fairly scurries along. This speed is partly achieved by the first two, quite complex, feet. They each have a suggestion of the amphibrach, and certainly the rhythm has a kind of triple foot rather than the two-stress pattern of the iamb. But metrical counting has little place in this verse of pause and hurry.

By and large, the rhythm speeds up as the poem progresses. This means that the address to the women, two-thirds of the way through, must be taken at quite a pace in the reading. As already indicated, the longer the line, the faster it goes:

»   ˘ ˘ ˘   ′ | ′ ˘|¶   ˘   ` ˘ ˘ |˘   ` ˘   ˘ ′ |

  Be not ashamed women . . . your privilege encloses the rest . . .

   ˘ ˘   ˘ ′ ˘|˘   ˘   ′ |

    it is the exit of the rest,

« ′ ˘   ˘| ′   ˘ ˘| ′ ˘|¶^   ˘   ˘   ˘| ′   ˘| ˘   ′ |

  You are the gates of the body   and you are the gates of the soul.

In the first of those two lines, there is the shadow of an amphi-brachic metre: 'your privilege encloses the rest'. In the second, as though in answer, there is the shadow of a dactylic metre: 'You are the gates of the body'. To prevent the line from falling into too metrical a pattern, it is necessary to place a stress of reasonable weight on 'and' rather than the second 'you': 'You are the gates of the body, *and* you are the gates of the soul'. The intonation is that of the orator rather than the expositor, and that is very much the tone characteristic of Whitman.

One need not be surprised, then, at finding that the ancillary sources for his rhythm, those other than the Bible, come from books of exhortation akin to speeches and sermons. We have, for instance, Whitman's explicit encomium on the radical freethinker Frances Wright (1795–1852) as 'a woman of the noblest make-up'. More than that, we have the tribute he paid her by imitating her style in his celebration of the art of public speaking, 'A Song of Joys':

> O the orator's joys!
> To inflate the chest, to roll the thunder of the voice out from the ribs and throat,
> To make the people rage, weep, hate, desire, with yourself.

The original of this was found by David Goodale (*American Literature*, May 1938) in Wright's *Views of Society and Manners in America*. Here she says that the orator should possess 'a voice full, sonorous, distinct, and flexible; exquisitely adapted to all the varieties of passion or argument'.

This is by no means the only parallel between Wright and Whitman. In *A Few Days in Athens* Wright recreates the sense of what it must have been like to have been addressed by Zeno, the founder of the Stoics:

> A crowd of disciples were assembled, waiting the arrival of their master. Some, crowded into groups, listened to the harangues of an elder or more able scholar . . . while innumerable single

figures, undisturbed by the buzz around them, leaned against
the pillars, studying each from a manuscript, or . . . wrapped in
silent meditation.

Wright is a powerful author, and it would not take too much to
put her descriptions into verse. Whitman, in fact, has done so, in
his poem 'Pictures':

Young men, pupils, collect in the gardens of a favorite master,
    waiting for him,
Some, crowded in groups, listen to the harangues or arguments
    of the elder ones,
Elsewhere, single figures, undisturbed by the buzz around them,
    lean against pillars, or within recesses, meditating, or studying
    manuscripts.

The resemblance, rhythmically as well as linguistically, is startling.
It is not that Whitman is prosaic, but rather than he drew sus-
tenance from examples of exalted prose.

Other instances that could be given include letters from John
Paul Jones to Benjamin Franklin, and *The Ruins* by the travel-
writer C. F. Volney (1757–1820), as translated by Volney himself
from the French in collaboration with Joel Barlow (1754–1812).
Here, the god Hermes is made to say: 'I have hitherto lived
banished from my true country; I now go back there. Do not weep
for me:/ I return to the celestial country whither every one goes in
his turn'. (A mark / to show the end of a cadence has been
inserted.) This is prose that itself has as a kind of sub-structure the
rhythms of the loose hexameter; that is to say, cadenced verse.
David Goodale, in the article already mentioned (see p. 107),
compares this prose with Whitman's poem, 'Salut au Monde':

Do not weep for me,
This is not my true country, I have lived banished from my true
    country, I now go back there,
I return to the celestial sphere where everyone goes in his turn.

As was the case with Eliot with respect to blank verse, Whitman had his predecessors who wrote in cadenced verse. Christopher Smart (1722–71) in his rhapsodic poem, *Jubilate Agno* (*Rejoice in the Lamb*) is one of them. William Blake, in his prophetic books, is another. As is the case with Whitman, Smart and Blake owed much to the Bible.

Also like Eliot, Whitman had successors. D. H. Lawrence (1885–1930), after beginning as a fairly traditional poet, wrote in that same long loose line that has been wrongly described as a form of excited prose. If one looks once more at 'I Sing the Body Electric' and then turns, say, to Lawrence's 'Tortoise Shout', the rhythmic connection is clear. Whitman has:

> Ebb stung by the flow, and flow stung by the ebb . . . loveflesh
>   swelling and deliciously aching,
> Limitless limpid jets of love hot and enormous . . . quivering jelly of
>   love . . . white-blow and delirious juice.

Now Lawrence, in lines from 'Tortoise Shout':

> Sex, which breaks us into voice, sets us calling across the deeps,
>   calling, calling for the complement,
> Singing, and calling, and singing again, being answered, having
>   found.
> Torn, to become whole again, after long seeking for what is lost,
> The same cry from the tortoise as from Christ, the Osiris-cry of
>   abandonment,
> That which is whole, torn asunder,
> That which is in part, finding its whole again throughout the
>   universe.

With the notable exception of Lawrence, Whitman's most effective influence has been upon American poets. Robert Bly (b. 1926; *American Poetry Review*, 1986) remarks: 'The greatness of this line no matter how rarely achieved, lies in its initial headlong rush and its powerful forward sweep, that resembles running animals with large chests. Its power comes also from the authority of those Hebraic–Elizabethan shouters whose voices penetrated our childhood chambers.' He illustrates this remark with an extract from a poem of his own, very much in Whitman's vein, 'The Teeth Mother Naked at Last':

> Lie after lie starts out into the prairie grass,
> like enormous caravans of Conestoga wagons . . .
> And a long desire for death flows out, guiding the enormous
>   caravans from beneath,
> stringing together the vague and foolish words.

Indeed, the most famous American poem of the mid-century – though not necessarily the best – is a rendering of Whitmanesque oratory: *Howl*, by Allen Ginsberg (b. 1926):

> I saw the best minds of my generation destroyed by madness,
>   starving hysterical naked,
> dragging themselves through the negro streets at dawn looking
>   for an angry fix . . .

If the reader says that the lines in each of these examples are not the same length, or that the scansion of each is not identical, both of those propositions are true. Such, however, is the nature of cadenced verse. The tendency is for each line to have six heavy stresses, but there can be lines that are shorter, for emphasis. So long as the forward movement is kept up, there can be almost any number of lightly stressed syllables and outrides. Of course, there are cases where the line collapses and we are, indeed, left with 'excited prose'. But that is to say that rhythm only works, in cadenced verse as in any other form of verse, when the poet is writing well.

Neither free blank verse nor cadenced verse should be confused with free verse proper. Free verse proper has its origin in blank verse, as is the case with the poetry of Eliot. But with free verse proper, the discrepancies and contrasts of the rhythm, rather than its forward movement, give rise to what is an essentially modern phenomenon.

Peter Redgrove (b. 1932), one of the best metrists of our time, put forward in correspondence with the present author a precursor of free verse. He cited a couple of lines from early Shakespeare. This is the Nurse speaking, in *Romeo and Juliet*:

For I had then laid wormwood to my dug,
Sitting in the sun under the dovehouse wall.

We notice that the first of these two lines is metrical in its effect, very much a formal iambic pentameter. The second line, although theoretically the same metre, subverts it. There is an extra syllable in the first foot, which thereby is rendered irregular, a dactyl ('sitting in') when one might have expected an iamb.

Then there is a heavy pause, not a mere caesura, after 'sun'. Further, in what – if the line were more regular – would be considered as the third foot, there is an inversion, 'under'. Thereby, the expected iamb is rendered as a trochee. If the line were taken by itself, it might very well be read as a variety of free verse. It is prevented, however, from taking off altogether from the iambic norm by the presence of the previous line, which is formal metrically. This is a predecessor of free verse; a prototype.

The two lines bear a relation, one to the other, akin to what in classical prosody is called *thesis* and *arsis*; that is to say, lowering and raising. The ancients applied these terms to the metrical foot. In their terminology, the more prominently rhythmic part of the foot was the *thesis*, and the less prominently rhythmic part of the foot was the *arsis*. In the present discussion, this contrast will be taken analogically, to apply not to the foot, but to the disposition of the lines in free verse proper.

Characteristically, as indicated in the discussion of cadenced verse, there is a line that thrusts, indicated thus », and a line that receives the thrust, indicated thus «. Sometimes it is one line pitted against two; sometimes the pattern is more complicated than that.

But, in the main, what makes for free verse proper, as distinct from free blank verse and (with some qualifications) cadenced verse, is the thrust of one line and the receptivity of another.

This mode of free verse existed as a special effect in the work of Milton, as witness the choruses in his tragedy *Samson Agonistes*. It also existed in the work of Matthew Arnold (1822–88), especially the speeches of the eponymous hero of his lyric drama *Empedocles on Etna*.

But free verse proper came into its own with the modernistic school of the early twentieth century. Though often written badly, and better considered as chopped-up prose, in the hands of a master such as Wallace Stevens, free verse proper becomes a recognizable form. The poem cited is called 'The Snow Man', and it is about empathy: feeling into a situation in order to understand it:

» One must have a mind of winter
« To regard the frost and the boughs
« Of the pine trees crusted with snow;

» And have been cold a long time
« To behold the junipers shagged with ice,
« The spruces rough in the distant glitter >

Of the January sun; » and not to think
» Of any misery in the sound of the wind,
« In the sound of a few leaves,

» Which is the sound of the land
« Full of the same wind
« That is blowing in the same bare place

« For the listener, who listens in the snow,
« And, nothing himself, beholds
« Nothing that is not there and the nothing that is.

What makes one line thrust, and another line prepared to receive the thrust? Basically, it is a question of the weight of the stress. In the first section of the poem, each line has a total of eight syllables. The first line, which thrusts, has three heavy stresses. The second and third lines, each of which receives the thrust, have two heavy stresses. Further, each of these two receiving lines begins with a series of light syllables:

» One must have a mind of winter

« To regard the frost and the boughs

« Of the pine trees crusted with snow . . .

This is not syllabics. The second section variegates the eight-syllable line, and there is no syllabic pattern running throughout. In the first line of this section, the heavy stresses fall on 'cold', 'long' and 'time', but the other stresses tend to be medium – 'been' – or medium-light – 'have'. So there is an aggregate of five stressed syllables to only two light ones – 'And', 'a'. This pattern gives the line a degree of weight. That enables it to thrust against the two successive lines, where only 'shagged' and 'rough' decisively bear a heavy stress:

» And have been cold a long   time

« To behold the junipers shagged with ice,

« The spruces rough in the distant glitter . . .

There is always room for debate in the scansion of free verse proper; that is a characteristic of free verse. What one does is propose a reading, not lay down a metrical grid. But it can be said that, in this second section, there is a scamper or scurry of lightly stressed syllables in such phrases as 'To behold the' and 'in the distant glitter'.

It is this tendency for the phrases to be lightly stressed, and therefore to travel with a greater degree of speed, that makes for receptivity to thrust. In a similar way, there is a tendency in a thrusting line to deploy a higher proportion of heavily stressed in relation to less heavily stressed syllables. Such a ratio of stressed syllables to light syllables slows the line down and gives an effect of weight.

What of the metrical length of the line? In free blank verse, as one would expect, there is a five-stress metre acting as the ground-work of the rhythm. In cadenced verse, while there may be five-stress lines, or short lines for emphasis, the tendency is to deploy a longer line, of six stresses or more; that which has been called a loose hexameter.

But in free verse proper a line can be of any length; accordant, that is to say, with the rhythmic pattern that is being set up in the poem. For example, William Carlos Williams (1883–1963) often chose to work in short lines. In 'The Widow's Lament in Springtime' there is set up a pattern of one thrusting line followed by a number of more lightly stressed line or lines to receive the thrust:

> » Sorrow is my own yard
> « where the new grass
> « flames as it has flamed
> « often before but not
> « with the cold fire
> « that closes round me this year.
> » Thirtyfive years
> « I lived with my husband.
> « The plumtree is white today
> « with masses of flowers.

» Masses of flowers
« load the cherry branches >
« and color some bushes
« yellow and some red
» but the grief in my heart
« is stronger than they
» for though they were my joy >
» formerly, « today I notice them
« and turn away forgetting.
» Today my son told me
« that in the meadows
« at the edge of the heavy woods
« in the distance he saw
« trees of white flowers. ¶
» I feel that I would like >
» to go there
« and fall into those flowers
« and sink into the marsh near them.

This is not identical in rhythmic pattern with the Stevens poem. But the disposition of free verse proper is not to repeat the exact rhythm from one poem to another. What should be noticed, however, is the relationship between heavily stressed lines that thrust and the more lightly stressed lines that receive that thrust.

The first line, 'Sorrow is my own yard', begins with a heavy stress on the first syllable. This is followed by syllables containing further heavy stresses on 'own' and 'yard'. That first line acts as a kind of propellant for the ensuing five lines. The impulse ebbs as these lines are spoken, until we have a dying fall on 'that closes round me this year'.

With the seventh line, 'Thirtyfive years' – three heavy stresses in no more than four syllables – the impulse reifies. It reifies; only once more to ebb. One notices the increase in the number of light and medium-light stresses in the succeeding three lines.

An interesting effect, showing how important context can be, is the way in which 'with masses of flowers', receptive of the now dying thrust, is turned in the very next line into a new thrust: 'Masses of flowers'. The mere dropping of the first syllable in this context transforms an iambic line, again with a dying fall, into a thrusting line, dactylic in nature, weighted enough to set onward a mini-series of three receptive lines.

Of course, this is not only a matter of rhythm. There is no matter of rhythm that can be disconnected from questions of diction or, indeed, questions of meaning and syntax. So any reading can be proposed only if we bear in mind these ancillary, and perhaps not so ancillary, elements.

In this poem, the widow is making a series of declarations: 'Sorrow is my own yard'; 'Thirtyfive years'; 'Masses of flowers'. The lines receiving these thrusts are in the nature of qualifiers. The declaration 'Sorrow is my own yard' is qualified by a series of modifying clauses. They indicate place: 'where the new grass/ . . . has flamed'. They also indicate time: 'often before'. Further, they admit of correction: 'but not with the cold fire'. All these are factors to be taken into account when scanning free verse proper.

Scansion is a rhythmic rather than a metrical affair. But rhythm is decided by tone of voice and the course of the argument. Redgrove, already quoted in this chapter, has a free-verse poem called 'Ghosts', describing a childless couple. It is metrically unlike the Williams poem in having much longer lines. Nevertheless, it maintains a not dissimilar rhythmic pattern, being shaped by the relationship between thrusting and receptive lines:

> » The terrace is said to be haunted.
> « By whom or what nobody knows; someone >
> « Put away under the vines behind dusty glass >
> « And rusty hinges staining the white-framed door >
> « Like a nosebleed, locked; or a death in the pond >
> « In three feet of water, a courageous breath?

» It's haunted anyway, so nobody mends it

« And the paving lies loose for the ants to crawl through

« Weaving and clutching like animated thorns.

» We walk on to it,

« Like the bold lovers we are, ten years of marriage,

» Tempting the ghosts out with our high spirits,

« Footsteps doubled by the silence . . .

» . . . and start up like ghosts ourselves

« Flawed lank and green in the greenhouse glass:

» She turns from that, and I sit down,

» She tosses the dust with the toe of a shoe,

» Sits on the pond's parapet and takes a swift look >

« At her shaking face in the clogged water,

« Weeds in her hair; »rises quickly and looks at me.

« I shrug, and turn my palms out, begin >

« To feel the damp in my bones as I lever up >

« And step towards her with my hints of wrinkles,

« Crows-feet and shadows. We leave arm in arm

» Not a word said. The terrace is haunted,

« Like many places with rough mirrors now,

« By estrangement, if the daylight's strong.

We can clearly see in this poem the practical working-out of Redgrove's own theory. The theory has already been evinced in his contrast between a more formally metrical and a less formally metrical line. Redgrove gave an example from *Romeo and Juliet* to indicate a kind of prototype free verse. His own verse here affords us a more advanced example.

The poem begins with a declaration, in line 1: 'The terrace is said to be haunted'. Here are three heavy stresses in nine syllables. The next five lines are a set of responses to this suggestion that the terrace is haunted. Line 2 says nobody knows by whom, but there is (line 3) the possibility of a body under the vines (4) behind rusty hinges, or else (5 and 6) someone having been drowned in an incongruously shallow pond.

With line 7, the declaration reasserts itself with a new thrust: 'It's haunted anyway, so nobody mends it'. The next two lines acquiesce to this, in descriptive detail of loose paving crawled through by animated ants.

That would be a sort of logical or thematic summing-up. But notice the rhythmic shape of the respective lines. 'The terrace is said to be haunted' is, in metrical terms, regular. But in rhythmic terms it is heavily stressed. The line is therefore emphatic. Those lines immediately following, so to speak, bow to that emphasis, with a greater number of lightly stressed syllables in relation to the heavy stresses:

˘ ` ˘ ` ´|˘ ˘ ´ |¶ ˘ ˘|>
By whom or what nobody knows, someone . . .

The effect in this answering line is one of acquiescence, a reassuring quality. The line, to retain the original terminology, is receptive of thrust.

Much the same could be said of the line following: 'Put away under the vines behind dusty glass'. Here we have a quantity of lightly stressed syllables, a paucity of heavily stressed ones. The receptive lines are, in other words, more complex in rhythm, less easily related to formal metrical feet. Further, those receptive lines tend to lead on to a set of enjambments: 'someone/Put away'; 'dusty glass/And rusty hinges'; 'the white-framed door/Like a nosebleed'.

There is an obvious contrast between the thrusting line, with its simple stressed shape, and the receptive lines that follow, with their more complicated shape replete with lightly stressed syllables. It is that contrast that gives this particular poem its pattern. Some such contrast is the basic form of free verse proper.

The form may be variegated. It is the nature of free verse to be variegated. But there is a limit to its extent of variation. If it loses the contrast of thrust and reception indicated here, free verse proper can degenerate into prose.

There are all too many examples of this. What can be said is that all free verse is difficult to write, and free verse proper is especially difficult. One may well be astonished that unpractised poets continue to attempt it, when forms more likely to bring success – sprung rhythm, pararhyme – lie so close to their hand.

The present author, in many years of writing, has himself achieved one example of free verse that satisfied his own ear. Perhaps the free verse was more appropriate on this occasion than on others, since the theme of the poem is that of the timorous soul who dares not venture into the unknown. It is called, perhaps with unconscious allusion to exhausted traditions, 'Dead End':

> We once lodged in that street.
> The roofs
> Beetled over the kerb,
> Glooming the narrow sidewalk. There
> Kids kicked listlessly at stones
> Between parked cars
> And dogs went on their business round the steps
> Where slatterns rasped.
>
> It never offered much. Even the sun
> Died on the upper windows.
>
> > But at the end,
> Like a stone curtain shutting off
> Another world, this wall.
> Beyond, green tops of trees
> Hinted at summer – almost we glimpsed
> Gables, pinnacles, domes,
> Even could guess at lawns
> Sloping to tinkling streams,
> Striplings at tennis, lithe girls sipping drinks . . .

For stuck
Bang in the forehead of that wall
– Where no stairs climbed, no ladder leaned –
A gate shut fast.
None of us ever saw it wide,
No one has passed right through –
For who would leave our street,
Its double banks of cars,
Sunless corners, listless kids
To peek, poke, pry
Beyond? What guarantee
Of leaves, flowering shrubs
And gardens, too, had we?
What if beyond
Stretched such another street
As ours, barren, run down?

But since we never tried the lock of that gate
To venture in
Leaving behind the world we knew
For one made new –
We never knew.

8

VERSE FORMS (I)

This chapter will seek to define some of the principal verse forms in English involving line groups of three or more.

Terza rima was invented by the Italian poet Dante for his vast work *La Divina Commedia*. It consists of three-line sections, interlinking one with another. The first and third lines of each section rhyme, and the second line rhymes with the first and third lines of the next section, thus: a b a b c b c d c d e d e f e. Any series of three-line sections, also known as tercets, may be brought to a conclusion by a single line rhyming with the second line of the three-line section immediately preceding. Dante wrote his sections in eleven-syllable lines, also termed hendecasyllabics.

In English, terza rima has been more discussed than practised. Chaucer introduced it in a minor poem, 'Complaint to his Lady'. However, a more influential exponent of this particular form was Sir Thomas Wyatt (1503–42). He was a contemporary and friend of the inventor of blank verse, the Earl of Surrey and, like him, was a close student of the Italians. Wyatt employed terza rima in his three satires, mostly complaining of life at court. The first is in the shape of a letter addressed to his friend, Sir John Poins (or Poyntz).

The metre is technically five-stress, but it is very much variegated into sprung rhythm:

Mine own John Poins, since ye delight to know
  The cause why that homeward I me draw,
And flee the press of courts whereso they go,

Rather than live thrall, under the awe
  Of lordly looks, wrapped within my cloak,
To will and lust learning to set a law;

It is not for because I scorn or mock
  The power of them, to whom fortune hath lent
Charge over us, of right, to strike the stroke:

But true it is that I have always meant
  Less to esteem them than the common sort
Of outward things that judge in their intent,

Without regard to what doth inward resort . . .

This 'powerful forward momentum', as *The New Princeton Encyclopedia of Poetry and Poetics* calls terza rima, renders it difficult to break off a quotation. 'It is a *perpetuum mobile* in which linkage and continuation are seamlessly articulated', the *Encyclopedia* continues.

Unfortunately, few poets in English have been able to maintain that forward momentum without considerably subverting the form. It was used by Sir Philip Sidney (1554–86), notably for the song of Lamon in his pastoral romance *Arcadia*: 'A shepherd's tale no height of style desires.' A nineteenth-century example is Lord Byron (1788–1824), who utilized it, appropriately enough, for his poem 'The Prophecy of Dante'.

The outstanding practitioner of this form in English, however, is Percy Bysshe Shelley (1792–1822). He was a good linguist and, especially, an *aficionado* of Italian verse. He attempted various versions of terza rima in his short career, always in lines of five stresses. *The Triumph of Life*, a poem on which he was working at the time of his death, shows the form at its fullest stretch. It is a vision which reveals multitudes of people being driven forward or else dragged along by a remorseless chariot:

> As in that trance of wondrous thought I lay,
> This was the tenor of my waking dream: –
> Methought I sat beside a public way
>
> Thick strewn with summer dust, and a great stream
> Of people there was hurrying to and fro,
> Numerous as gnats upon the evening gleam,
>
> All hastening onward, yet none seemed to know
> Whither he went, or whence he came, or why
> He made one of the multitude, yet so
>
> Was borne amid the crowd, as through the sky,
> One of the million leaves of summer's bier;
> Old age and youth, manhood and infancy,
>
> Mixed in one mighty torrent did appear . . .

The method seems to be *not* to close the sentence at the end of a section. Indeed, this extract quoted is part of a mighty sentence that goes on (the texts are disputed) for either seven or else nine sections more. Unfinished though the poem is, and fragmented though some of the lines are, the impetus hardly ever wanes.

There is no parallel in modern times. T. S. Eliot attracted acclaim for what was felt to be a Dantesque passage in 'Little Gidding'. However, the passage in question can hardly be termed terza rima, since it does not rhyme. Indeed, a section of it has already been adduced, in the previous chapter, as, in part, redolent of the English playwright Cyril Tourneur. The scene records a dialogue between two poets in an air raid during the Second World War:

> In the uncertain hour before the morning
>> Near the ending of interminable night
>> At the recurrent end of the unending
> After the dark dove with the flickering tongue
>> Had passed below the horizon of his homing
>> While the dead leaves still rattled on like tin
> Over the asphalt where no other sound was . . .

One could say that a certain effect approximating to that of terza rima is obtained by the use of feminine endings; that is to say, ends of lines finishing on a light syllable. These may be held to approximate to Dante's eleven-syllable or hendecasyllabic lines. In Eliot, they alternate with five-stress lines ending on a strong syllable.

Thus, in the extract above, we can see that 'morning' and 'ending', the first and second lines of the first tercet, act as a sort of a-rhyme. In the second line, 'night' corresponds in some sort to a b-rhyme attaching itself to 'tongue' and 'tin', the rhyme words of the first and third lines of the second tercet.

The dialogue in 'Little Gidding' has been influential in interposing itself between terza rima as practised by English poets of the past and the practice of the moderns. Seamus Heaney, referred to in Chapter 1 as a distinguished metrist, has developed a highly personal form of terza rima. In his sequence 'Station Island', the connection with Eliot is clear enough. The scene he describes is essentially, like that of Eliot, a dialogue between two writers. In the present case, the writers are William Carleton (1794–1869) and Heaney himself:

> I was parked on a high road, listening
> to peewits and wind blowing round the car
> when something came to life in the driving mirror,

> someone walking fast in an overcoat
> and boots, bareheaded, big, determined
> in his sure haste along the crown of the road
>
> so that I felt myself the challenged one . . .

Probably we would not feel this to be even an echo of terza rima were it not for Eliot's interposition between the past use of the form and the present. Heaney has considerably developed this usage of the form in his later verse.

There is a translation of Dante in Heaney's book *Seeing Things* which achieves something of a terza rima effect by pararhyming the first and third lines of each tercet, and leaving each second line unrhymed. The echo of the terza rima is fainter in a sequence of twelve-lined poems, each arranged as four tercets, called 'Lightenings'. Really, the form in Heaney's hands deserves a name of its own. It would seem to have left the essentially linked tercets of Wyatt and Shelley well behind. The final poem in the sequence, 'xxxvi', would hardly be differentiated from free blank verse were it not for the tercet-like arrangement of its lines:

> And yes, my friend, we too walked through a valley,
> Once. In darkness. With all the streetlamps off.
> As danger gathered and the march dispersed.
>
> Scenes from Dante, made more memorable
> By one of his head-clearing similes –
> Fireflies, say, since the policemen's torches
>
> Clustered and flicked . . .

It is probable that a stricter version of terza rima, like a number of forms in English that began as tightly rhymed patterns, can be truly effective in the later twentieth century only in parodic or satirical circumstances.

Much more central to the tradition of English verse is the four-line stanza rhyming a b a b, the lines themselves being five-stressed. It has been harnessed to several different functions.

This metrical pattern began as a stanza suitable for romance and for heroic poetry. Notable early examples include *Nosce teipsum*, a poem about the nature of man, by Sir John Davies (1569–1626), and the fragmentary 'The Ocean to Cynthia', a love poem to Queen Elizabeth by Sir Walter Raleigh (?1554–1618). In the mid-seventeenth century, there was *Gondibert*, a romantic epic of some seven thousand lines by Sir William D'Avenant (1606–68). Even more than D'Avenant, John Dryden, in his *Annus mirabilis*, brought this particular stanza into prominence.

Dryden's poem in part concerns the battles at sea between the Dutch and the British (under the Duke of Albemarle), in 1666:

Among the Dutch thus Albemarle did fare:
  He could not conquer and disdained to fly:
Past hope of safety, 'twas his latest care
  Like falling Caesar, decently to die.

Yet pity did his manly spirit move,
  To see those perish who so well had fought;
And, generously, with his despair he strove,
  Resolved to live till he their safety wrought.

These are just two stanzas from a fairly long poem. But they should be enough to show that, whatever else it can do, this stanza is not best fitted for heroic narrative. The fault does not lie with Dryden's personality. He was to show himself capable of heroic flights on other occasions, most notably in the couplets of his tragedy *Aurung-Zebe*, and his translations from Virgil and Homer.

There is, however, a degree of propensity in-built with regard to any given verse form. The stanza Dryden used in *Annus mirabilis* is virtually incapable of moving quickly, partly because it tends to come to a halt at the end of the fourth line. The alternating rhymes, too, have the effect of slowing the rhythm up. That is why the stanza is not really suitable for tales of battle and heroism.

The next phase in the development of this stanza proved to be a vehicle for quasi-satiric meditation. There is a poem, 'The Maimed Debauchee', by the Earl of Rochester (1647–80). A sequence of naval and military metaphors is utilized to assemble what amounts to a derisive answer to *Annus mirabilis*. The subject is that of an old lecher retired from the fray but encouraging younger adventurers to emulate his exploits:

> Should hopeful youths (worth being drunk) prove nice,
> And from their fair inviters meanly shrink,
> 'Twould please the ghost of my departed vice,
> If at my counsel they repent and drink.
>
> Or should some cold-complexioned sot forbid,
> With his dull morals, our night's brisk alarms,
> I'll fire his blood by telling what I did,
> When I was strong and able to bear arms.
>
> I'll tell of whores attacked, their lords at home,
> Bawds' quarters beaten up, and fortress won,
> Windows demolished, watches overcome,
> And handsome ills by my contrivance done.

The 'watches' are the bands of watchmen or vigilantes, sometimes aged or infirm, who volunteered or were drafted to keep the peace. They were often defeated by the vigorous young aristocrats who frequented the Court of Charles II.

Rochester's satire was imitated in a poem, called simply 'Stanzas', from the pen of the notorious politician John Sheffield, Duke of Buckinghamshire (1649–1721). He contemplates his tortuous life with ironic satisfaction, using the heroic stanza to describe his own unheroic figure:

Then, as old lechers in a winter's night
  To yawning hearers all their pranks disclose:
And what decay deprives them of delight,
  Supply with vain endeavours to impose:

Just so shall I as idly entertain
  Some stripling patriots, fond of seeming wise;
Tell, how I still could great employments gain,
  Without concealing truths, or whispering lies!

Heroism was pushed even further away from this particular stanza by James Hammond (1710–42), in a posthumously published sequence called *Love Elegies*. Though Hammond's poems were not elegies in the sense usually accepted, that of commemorating a departed friend, nevertheless they had the pivotal effect of moving the four-line stanza into an elegiac mood. For, though these poems purport to treat of love, their underlying subject is death.

Here is a stanza from Elegy V:

At her command the vigorous summer pines,
And wintery clouds obscure the hopeful year;
At her strong bidding, gloomy winter shines,
And vernal roses on the snows appear.

Here is a stanza from Elegy XII:

With thee in gloomy deserts let me dwell,
Where never human footstep marked the ground;
Thou, light of life, all darkness canst expel,
And seem a world with solitude around.

This sounded a new note in English poetry. Especially, these poems anticipate the work of Thomas Gray (1716–71), who most of all put the four-line stanza in stage centre. The definitive version of the stanza, thereafter to be called the 'elegiac stanza', is to be found in Gray's 'Elegy written in a Country Church-Yard'. The various sections are held together not by a plot, but by the prevailing mood of settled melancholy. This, in no small measure, is brought about by the peculiar intonation Gray gives what had been the heroic stanza. Stanza 14 reads:

> Full many a gem of purest ray serene
>> The dark unfathomed caves of ocean bear:
> Full many a flower is born to blush unseen,
>> And waste its sweetness on the desert air.

There is a slowness of rhythm largely brought about by the stasis at the end of every fourth line, and by the alternating rhymes. The poem begins, most memorably:

> The curfew tolls the knell of parting day,
>> The lowing herd wind slowly o'er the lea,
> The ploughman homeward plods his weary way,
>> And leaves the world to darkness and to me.

> Now fades the glimmering landscape on the sight,
>> And all the air a solemn stillness holds,
> Save where the beetle wheels his droning flight,
>> And drowsy tinklings lull the distant folds.

This verse-pattern is far better suited to the topic of Gray's 'Elegy' – untimely death and oblivion – than it was to the heroics of *Annus mirabilis*. It lends itself to a subdued quality of speech.

Wordsworth used the form in his 'Elegiac Stanzas suggested by a Picture of Peele Castle', written in memory of his brother John, who was drowned at sea:

> How perfect was the calm! it seemed no sleep;
> No mood, which season takes away, or brings:
> I could have fancied that the mighty deep
> Was even the gentlest of all gentle things.

One cannot say that this use of the stanza settled the form of the elegy for ever. Nevertheless, a number of poets found the stanza congenial, not only as a way of memorializing their departed friends, but as a mode of meditative lyric. In the nineteenth century, there were variations such as Emily Brontë's mainly trochaic 'Cold in the earth, and the deep snow piled above thee', and also the *Rubáiyát of Omar Khayyám* by Edward Fitzgerald with its stanza rhyming a a b a.

In the twentieth century, Gray's elegiac stanza was put to use to meditative effect by some of the so-called Georgians; that is to say, poets of the reign of George V. These included W. H. Davies (1861–1940; see his poem, 'Days that have Been'), Walter de la Mare (1873–1956; see 'Beyond') and W. J. Turner (1889–1946; see 'Peace').

Later on in the century, the stanza once more became the vehicle for quasi-satirical meditations. William Empson (1906–84) made notable use of it in such poems as 'To an Old Lady', 'Letter II' and 'Legal Fiction'. He was much imitated. We can find sentiments expressed in Empson's purged manner, and in that stanza, by such writers as Kingsley Amis (b. 1922; see his poem 'Wrong Words'); Donald Davie (b. 1922; see 'Remembering the Thirties'); and Robert Conquest (b. 1917; see 'The Rokeby Venus'). An alternative stanza, rhyming a b b a, is almost as often employed, and seems interchangeable with the elegiac stanza proper.

A stanza also used for elegy, but with a different provenance, is what is now called the *In Memoriam* stanza. The lines rhyme a b b a as is the case with the alternative elegiac stanza, but they are a foot shorter, being in tetrameters. The stanza in question did not originate with the author of *In Memoriam* but with a love poem by Ben Jonson, 'An Elegy':

> Though beauty be the mark of praise,
>   And yours of whom I sing be such
>   As not the world can praise too much,
> Yet is't your virtue now I raise.

A virtue, like alloy, so gone
   Throughout your form: as though that move,
   And draw, and conquer all men's love,
This subjects you to love of one.

Wherein you triumph yet: because
   'Tis of yourself, and that you use
   The noblest freedom, not to choose
Against or faith or honour's laws.

The stanza seems to embody a built-in dying fall. The voice takes each line a shade lower in pitch until the final line of the stanza reaches a low point. Then, with the next stanza, the voice rises at the first line, but not quite so high as in the preceding stanza, and the last line is, consequently, a little lower in pitch than the preceding last line.

Pitch is notoriously hard to determine, for it is the matter of *all* matters that each reader will interpret in an individual way. Yet the approach suggested here should be found to make most sense of a stanza whose peculiar virtue is not only to produce a mood of gentle melancholy, but also to be remarkably suitable for reasoning in verse.

Both qualities, melancholy and reasoning power, are manifest in 'An Ode upon a Question Moved, whether Love should continue for ever?' by Lord Herbert of Cherbury (1582–1648):

Having interred her infant-birth,
   The watery ground that late did mourn,
   Was strewed with flowers for the return
Of the wished bridegroom of the earth.

The well-accorded birds did sing
   Their hymns unto the pleasant time,
   And in a sweet consorted chime
Did welcome in the cheerful spring.

> To which, soft whistles of the wind,
>   And warbling murmurs of a brook,
>   And varied notes of leaves that shook,
> An harmony of parts did bind.
>
> While doubling joy unto each other,
>   All in so rare consent was shown,
>   No happiness that came alone
> Nor pleasure that was not another.

The poem goes on, for another thirty-one mellifluous stanzas, debating the possibility of mutual recognition by two lovers after death. ('Consent', by the way, here means consensus or accord.)

The stanza was not taken up again, however, until Alfred, Lord Tennyson. He gave the stanza its name by using it as the vehicle of his immense elegiac poem *In Memoriam*. The poem itself is amorphous, being in fact a series of elegies for Tennyson's friend, Arthur Henry Hallam (1811–33). This untimely death gave a focus to a constitutional melancholy that had beset Tennyson's poems from a very early date. The specific rhythm he brought out of the stanza is mesmeric. Here is section VII:

> Dark house, by which once more I stand
>   Here in the long unlovely street,
>   Doors, where my heart was used to beat
> So quickly, waiting for a hand,
>
> A hand that can be clasped no more –
>   Behold me, for I cannot sleep,
>   And like a guilty thing I creep
> At earliest morning to the door.
>
> He is not here; but far away
>   The noise of life begins again,
>   And ghastly through the drizzling rain
> On the bald street breaks the blank day.

Probably because of that impressive usage, the *In Memoriam* stanza has been little employed since 1850, when this was first published. The problem with highly distinctive patterns of verse, like the *In Memoriam* stanza, is that any poem using the same form is liable to seem an echo or even parody of the prototype. Oscar Wilde (1854–1900) essayed a few examples, but none of his attempts – 'Impression du Matin', 'Le Jardin' – seems to have reached the anthologies. A modern instance is Larkin's 'The Trees', in *High Windows*.

There is also the Horatian stanza, which is an attempt to domesticate in English the form adopted for his odes by the Roman poet Horace (65–8 BC). This consists of four-line stanzas, in which the first two lines are longer than the second two lines. The stanza can be patterned as as two tetrameters followed by two trimeters, or as two pentameters followed by two tetrameters. Sometimes the stanza rhymes a a b b, as in 'An Horatian Ode upon Cromwell's Return from Ireland' by Andrew Marvell. This begins:

> The forward youth that would appear
> Must now forsake his Muses dear,
>   Nor in the shadows sing
>   His numbers languishing.

Sometimes the stanza is unrhymed, and this can produce a curiously obsessional effect, as in 'The Ode to Evening' by William Collins (1721–59). It begins:

> If aught of oaten stop or pastoral song,
> May hope, chaste Eve, to soothe thy modest ear,
>   Like thine own solemn springs,
>   Thy springs and dying gales . . .

and on and on in an immense sentence which lasts for four more stanzas. This poem influenced the rise of Romanticism in the eighteenth century. In turn its predecessor, the 'Horatian Ode' by Marvell, has been acclaimed as the greatest political poem in the language. The examples of this stanza in action, though illustrious, have given rise to few effective imitations.

On the whole, it is the less distinctive verse forms that have the longest cycles of employment. The usual stanza for hymns, those lyrics sung as part of a church service, has given rise to much good but little great writing. If one looks through such a compilation as *Hymns Ancient and Modern*, most of the contributions are in four-line stanzas, with lines of alternating four stresses and three stresses, rhyming a b a b. The earliest among the original compositions, as distinct from translated works, are written by Isaac Watts (1674–1748). The beginning of one of his most famous hymns will give some sense of the hymn stanza:

> Our God, our help in ages past,
>   Our hope in years to come,
> Our shelter from the stormy blast,
>   And our eternal home.
>
> Under the shadow of thy throne
>   Thy saints have dwelt secure;
> Sufficient is thine arm alone,
>   And thy defence is sure.
>
> Before the hills in order stood,
>   Or earth received her frame,
> From everlasting thou art God,
>   To endless years the same.

The language is unforced, but not distinguished. It is highly suitable, therefore, for being sung. But, whether performed or not, the hymns provided many examples of song in the early and middle eighteenth century, a period not on the whole remarkable for lyric impulse. One of the most prolific hymn-writers was Charles Wesley (1707–88):

O for a thousand tongues to sing
  My dear Redeemer's praise,
The glories of my God and King,
  The triumphs of his grace!

Jesus! the name that charms our fears,
  That bids our sorrows cease;
'Tis music in the sinner's ears,
  'Tis life and health and peace.

He speaks; and, listening to his voice,
  New life the dead receive,
The mournful broken hearts rejoice,
  The humble poor believe.

This is the beginning of a lyric that in itself may seem modest enough. However, as set to the anonymous tune in Isaac Smith's *Collection*, and when sung by a trained choir in the context of a medieval cathedral, the impact is considerable. This is to suggest that, however well turned the verse of a hymn may be, the form is really a mixed genre and cannot be judged by the words upon the page. It is a product of performance.

A frequent variant of the hymn stanza is one where the basic form acquires a rhyming couplet in four-stress lines. The following example, also by Charles Wesley, further extends the form by being written in trochaic rather than iambic verse, and in tetrameters throughout. Here is the first stanza:

Christ, whose glory fills the skies,
  Christ, the true, the only Light,
Sun of righteousness, arise,
  Triumph o'er the shades of night;
Daypring from on high, be near;
Daystar, in my heart appear.

William Cowper (1731–1800) was one of the few poets of distinction to make use of the hymn stanza. Moments of vision may be found in hymns such as 'Sometimes a light surprises', 'God moves in a mysterious way', and 'O for a closer walk with God'.

Cowper's greatest single poem, while being closely linked to the tradition as defined by Watts and Wesley, is nevertheless a subversion of the hymn stanza. Metrically, it is the six-line variant as already defined. It has the normal alternation of four stresses and three stresses, and the alternating rhyme a b a b, with the addition of a rhyming couplet in four-stress lines. The rhythmic effect, however, goes well beyond this description. We are conscious of being very near a suffering conscience. One could not imagine this poem being sung, in church or anywhere else. The poem is all the more powerful for allegorizing the victim's sense of loss. It ostensibly tells of a sailor lost overboard in a storm. Really, however, this is a representation of anxiety encroaching to the point of suicide. The poem in question is called 'The Castaway'. It begins:

> Obscurest night involved the sky,
>   The Atlantic billows roared,
> When such a destined wretch as I
>   Washed headlong from on board,
> Of friends, of hope, of all bereft,
> His floating home forever left.
>
> No braver chief could Albion boast
>   Than he with whom he went,
> Nor ever ship left Albion's coast,
>   With warmer wishes sent.
> He loved them both, but both in vain,
> Nor him beheld, nor her again.
>
> Not long beneath the whelming brine,
>   Expert to swim he lay;

Nor soon he felt his strength decline
  Or courage die away;
But waged with death a lasting strife,
Supported by despair of life.

('Albion' is the ancient name for Britain, derived from the white cliffs which distinguish some of its coasts.) One effect of the poem is partly owing to a kind of intellectual counterpoint. The reader cannot forget the hymn stanza on which this surging rhythm is based, yet the rhythm itself has a speed and urgency which would be impossible in a hymn. The language is taut and precise; not at all the conventional diction seemly in a house of prayer.

The hymn stanza went on its way in spite of this intervention on Cowper's part. Reginald Heber (1773–1833), John Keble (1792–1866) and Christina Rossetti (1830–94) all wrote hymns approaching the condition of poetry, and the last-named may be held to have achieved it. With the decay of organized religion in the twentieth century, naturally the use of the various hymn stanzas declined. There are few, if any, modern hymns to equal the eighteenth-century ones. Nevertheless, in the 1970s and 1980s, a hymn by Cowper's friend John Newton (1725–1807) was played and sung almost everywhere. Significantly, perhaps, this phenomenon, called 'Amazing Grace', did not occur in *Hymns Ancient and Modern*.

In the twentieth century, the hymn stanza has been employed for mildly satiric purposes, most notably, perhaps, by the predecessor of Ted Hughes as Poet Laureate, Sir John Betjeman (1906–84); see, for example, his 'Portrait of a Deaf Man'. However, the hymn stanza has an *alter ego*. So far as metrical scansion goes, there is no difference between the hymn stanza and ballad metre. Rhythmically, however, they are quite distinct.

The point can be made if we consider a line from Wesley:

  ´ ˘|˘ ^ |˘ ´ | ˘ ` |>
  O for a thousand tongues to sing . . .

or a line from Cowper:

´ ˘ | ˘ ^ | ˘ ` | ˘ ´ |

O for a closer walk with God . . .

There is certainly a family resemblance between these hymns.

The rhythm of the ballad sets up quite a different pattern. For one thing, the heavy stresses and the lighter stresses are much more sharply differentiated in the ballad than in the hymn. There are more heavy stresses in relation to the total number of syllables in each line. There are also fewer medium and medium-light stresses. Whatever is not heavily stressed in the ballad tends to be either lightly stressed or unstressed, in the manner of outrides.

Here are three representative stanzas from ballads; in each case, the stanza is the first in the poem:

> There lived a wife at Usher's Well
>   And a wealthy wife was she;
> She had three stout and stalwart sons,
>   And sent them o'er the sea . . .
>   ('The Wife of Usher's Well')

> The King sits in Dunfermline town,
>   Drinking the blood-red wine:
> 'O where will I get good sailor,
>   To sail this ship of mine . . . ?'
>   ('Sir Patrick Spens')

> 'O where have you been, my long, long love,
>   This long seven years and more?'
> 'O I'm come to seek my former vows
>   Ye granted me before . . . '
>   ('James Harris')

As was the case with the hymns, these stanzas resemble one another. They resemble one another in being dramatic, almost abrupt, in utterance, and in conveying a sense of excitement. There is no preamble, no sense of meditation, not a wasted word. This conciseness and momentum are a property of the rhythm:

   ˇ   ˊ | ˇ ˊ | ˇ ˊ |ˇ   ˊ |>

There lived a wife at Usher's Well . . .

   ˇ   ˊ | ˊ ˇ| ˇ   ˊ | ˇ   ˊ |

The King sits in Dunfermline town . . .

  ˇ   ˊ | ˇ   ˇ   ˊ | ˇ ˊ | ˇ   ˊ |

'O where have you been, my long, long love . . . '?

The rhythm is made for speed. In this last example, one would expect a slowing-down because of the succession of stressed syllables in the last phrase, 'long, long love'. But the line is sprung by the anapaest in the second foot. The result is that the rhythm comes down on a heavy stress on the first 'long' – so heavy, in fact, that the reader lingers on that first 'long' and, in defiance of what out of context might be expected, leaps over the second 'long' to preserve momentum.

Thus it is with practically all ballads. They emerged in medieval times, well before the earliest manuscripts and seem to have been primarily an oral form; probably sung, rather than spoken. Characteristically, they are anonymous; songs of the folk rather than of one named poet. The ballads that show signs of lingering and meditation are the later ones, such as 'The Unquiet Grave', which is probably a product of the eighteenth century. It begins:

> The wind doth blow today, my love,
>> And a few small drops of rain:
> I never had but one true love,
>> In cold grave she was lain . . .

This is more song than ballad. As with the hymns, there seems to be less differentiation between stressed and more lightly stressed syllables. Further, there is a degree of likeness rhythmically between this and productions of art (rather than folk) in the nineteenth century, such as 'Porphyria's Lover' by Robert Browning. This latter begins:

> The rain set early in tonight,
>> The sullen wind was soon awake,
> It tore the elm-tops down for spite,
>> And did its worst to vex the lake:
>> I listened with heart fit to break . . .

As the comparison will suggest, the ballad was much imitated by middle-class poets. But it was usually the more sophisticated ballads, such as 'The Unquiet Grave', that were imitated, with the imitations having a distinguishing factor of more complex rhythm, and often an input of meditative comment.

The most astonishing imitation of ballad form was written by Samuel Taylor Coleridge, whose inventiveness of metre we looked at in Chapter 5, on sprung verse. *The Rime of the Ancient Mariner* is very much a literary production. The theme of a sailor in peril at sea was suggested to Coleridge by Wordsworth in 1797. At that time Coleridge had never even been on a ship, let alone voyaged to the exotic climes of his projected poem. The next few months were devoted to a frenzied search through numerous travel books which, in the end, served as the raw material of *The Ancient Mariner*, and the rhythmic impulse certainly came from the ballads of the Scottish Border. 'Sir Patrick Spens' has:

> Late late yestreen I saw the new moon
>> With the old moon in her arm,
> And I fear, I fear, my dear master,
>> That we will come to harm.

In Coleridge the stanza is often extended. Further, those opportunities for pararhyme that were ignored in the simple directness of the old ballad are here fully exploited:

We listened and looked sideways up!
Fear at my heart, as at a cup,
My life-blood seemed to sip!
The stars were dim, and thick the night,
The steersman's face by his lamp gleamed white;
From the sails the dew did drip –
Till clomb above the eastern bar
The horned Moon, with one bright star
Within the nether tip.

Literary recensions of the ballads were part of the onset of Romanticism. What to many littérateurs in the eighteenth century had seemed barbaric, now became the basis of art-speech. One has only to think of Sir Walter Scott's 'Proud Maisie', Keats's 'La Belle Dame sans Merci', 'A Nuptial Eve' by Sydney Dobell (1824–74) with its refrain 'O Keith of Ravelston,/The sorrows of thy line', and 'The Ballad of Reading Gaol' by Oscar Wilde.

Something in the ballad, however, stubbornly refuses to be imitated. Its loyalty to the austere ballad stanza retains a vivacity that is denied to the poets who have sought to learn from it – unless at the same time they divagate into more elaborate forms and more sophisticated language, and so lose some sense of their original.

This deracination never took place to the same extent in the Scots tongue, a development parallel with English: more than a dialect, though less than a separate language. As well as an abundant use of the ballad stanza, a kind of variant upon that stanza arose. It was called the Habbie stanza, after one of the earliest usages, 'The Epitaph of Habbie Stimson' or 'The Life and Death of the Piper of Kilbarchan' by Sir Robert Sempill of Beltrees (?1595–?1660). The form of the stanza is three iambic tetrameters rhyming a a a; then a dimeter, sometimes amphibrachic, carrying a b-rhyme; then a further tetrameter, rhyming with the three foregoing; then a concluding dimeter, rhyming with the previous dimeter:

> Kilbarchan now may say alas!
> For she hath lost her game and grace,
> Both Trixie and the Maiden Trace:
>   But what remead?
> For no man can supply his place,
>   Hab Simson's dead.

The Habbie stanza came to its greatest strength in the Scots revival of the eighteenth century, pioneered by Allan Ramsay (1686–1758). Ramsay used the form for mildly facetious purposes ('Lucky Spence's Last Advice'), as did his friend William Hamilton of Gilbertfield (1665–1751), who put it into the mouth of a dying greyhound.

However, in the hands of a short-lived poet of rare talent, it became a vehicle for genuine poetry. Robert Fergusson (1750–74) was author of 'The Daft-Days' and 'To the Tron-Kirk Bell'. Such works as these inspired Robert Burns (1759–96) to produce some of his greatest poems. They include his 'Address to the De'il', 'To a Louse', the epistles to John Lapraik and other fellow-poets, and also his attack on the 'salvation by faith and not works' brand of Christianity, 'Holy Willie's Prayer'. It begins:

> O Thou that in the Heavens dost dwell,
> Wha, as it pleases best Thysel',
> Sends ane to heaven and ten to Hell
>   A' for thy glory,
> And no for ony guid or ill
>   They've done afore Thee!

The stanza in this poem rattles along with zest and speed. But Burns can also make it a vehicle for quiet meditation, as in 'To a Mouse', which begins:

> Wee, sleekit, cow'rin', tim'rous beastie,
> O, what a panic's in thy breastie!
> Thou need na start awa sae hasty

> Wi' bickering brattle!
> I wad be laith to rin and chase thee,
> Wi' murd'ring pattle!

('Brattle' is 'squeaking', and a 'pattle' is a paddle or plough-staff.) A number of English poets, notably Wordsworth, imitated what by then was known as the Burns stanza. It never in their hands, however, achieved the *élan* that Burns gave it. The stanza has, perhaps significantly, played little part in the twentieth-century revival of Scots peculiarly associated with the name of Hugh MacDiarmid (1892–1978).

Another offshoot of the ballad is what George Saintsbury, Victorian prosodist, called 'the ineffable cadence' (see the edition of Katherine Philips,1631–64, in his *Caroline Poets*). This was in effect started off by Ben Jonson, himself of Border descent, who has (for example) a poem breathing the uncertainty of new love in a stanza, paradoxically, of matchless assurance:

> Oh do not wanton with those eyes
> Lest I be sick with seeing,
> Nor cast them down, but let them rise
> Lest shame destroy their being.

Poems such as this helped to start off the Cavalier lyric, which was such a feature of the seventeenth century. Sidney Godolphin (1610–43) has:

> No more unto my thoughts appear,
> At least appear less fair,
> For crazy tempers justly fear
> The goodness of the air.

Sir John Suckling (1609–41) was a leading member of the Royalist party and imported a note of stoic confidence into Cavalier poetry:

> I prithee send me back my heart,

> Since I cannot have thine:
> For if from yours you will not part,
> Why then shouldst thou have mine?

This metrical form of alternating four-stress and three-stress lines remained in favour through the eighteenth and nineteenth centuries, and well into the twentieth. Its dance-like quality received a boost through the popularity of *A Shropshire Lad*, a poem cycle by A. E. Housman, whose work was mentioned in Chapter 4 with regard to the song-lyric.

Nevertheless, the ballads from which the Cavalier lyric stemmed remain an inspiration to modern poets, along with even more fundamental forms, such as the spell and the nursery rhyme. In his book of essays *On the Poet and his Craft* (Seattle, 1965) the American poet Theodore Roethke (1908–63) quotes a rhyme:

> Hinx, minx, the old witch winks!
> The fat begins to fry!
> There's nobody home but Jumping Joan,
> And father, and mother, and I.

He applauds its catchiness, its sprung rhythm, but does not mention that there is an equivalent on this side of the Atlantic:

> Quick, quick,
> The cat's been sick.
> Where? Where?
> Under the chair.
> Hasten, hasten,
> Fetch the basin.
> Kate, Kate
> You're far too late.

Why is one of these an equivalent of the other? The subject-matter would seem to be quite disparate. But the sounds are much the same: 'Hinx, minx, the old witch winks' and 'Quick, quick,/

The cat's been sick' are rhythmically very similar. Iona and Peter Opie in their book *The Lore and Language of Schoolchildren* (Oxford, 1959) show how a similar rhythm can spark off quite different sets of words.

Some of the most apparently mysterious poems in the language are quite functional, if only one is willing to listen to them. There is a medieval carol:

> Maiden in the moor lay,
>   In the moor lay,
> Seven nights full, seven nights full,
> Maiden in the moor lay,
>   In the moor lay.
> Seven nights full and a day.
>
> Well was her meat.
>   What was her meat?
>   The primrose and the –
>   The primrose and the –
> Well was her meat.
> What was her meat?
>   The primrose and the violet.

– and so on. The late E. M. W. Tillyard could be heard in the Mill Lane lecture rooms of 1950s Cambridge making heavy weather concerning the symbolic content of this anonymous poem. But, in fact, if one listens to it, 'Maiden in the moor lay' will take shape as a child's skipping-song. This does not, however, detract from its haunting quality. What many of these folk-rhymes have is magic.

It is a quality coveted by sophisticated poets. Another rhyme goes:

> I am of Ireland
> And of the holy land

> Of Ireland.
> Good sir, pray I thee,
> For of saint charity,
> Come and dance with me
> In Ireland.

W. B. Yeats got hold of this fugitive piece, and turned it into an unsatisfactory art poem. He added motivation – '"And time runs on," cried she.' He added an amount of grotesque detail – 'The fiddlers are all thumbs,/Or the fiddle-string accursed.' What Yeats lost, great poet as he was, was the simplicity and the magic. He supplied a narrative context for a piece whose singular charm is to have no context.

Mostly, nursery rhymes, skipping-songs and similar flotsam have short sprung lines. The sound seems to govern the sense. Not many of them are genuine poetry, though most of them are (to use Roethke's term) 'catchy'.

It is the rare poet who can build upon them without embellishing the original forms out of existence. The attempts made in this direction by Theodore Roethke, fine lyricist though he was, tend to be functionlessly eccentric. Much of the effect, when such imitations come off, stems from making do without the artifices of metropolitan craft. James Stephens (1880–1950) and Walter de la Mare are two poets who can write in such a fashion that there is sometimes no way of telling whether the poem in question is grounded upon a piece of folk-song or an emanation from the poet's own art. Such a work is de la Mare's 'The Song of the Mad Prince'. It begins:

> Who said 'Peacock Pie'?
>   The old King to the sparrow:
> Who said, 'Crops are ripe'?
>   Rust to the harrow:
> Who said 'Where sleeps she now?
>   Where rests she now her head,

Bathed in eve's loveliness?'
  That's what I said.

The rhythm is almost as guileless that of a skipping-song. Yet there are overtones of *Hamlet* and *King Lear* – both plays full of singing – that arise strangely from the child-like rhyme.

The poet who can do this sort of thing consummately is Stevie Smith (1902–71). Critics have had a hard time with her work, because she corresponds to very few of the expectations with which a twentieth-century poet is usually approached. The approach on the critic's part must be to listen.

The apparently simple rhythms of Smith are a little trickier than they seem on the page. Consider 'My Cats':

> I like to toss him up and down
> A heavy cat weighs half a Crown
> With a hey ho diddle my cat Brown.
>
> I like to pinch him on the sly
> When nobody is passing by
> With a hey ho diddle my cat Fry.
>
> I like to ruffle up his pride
> And watch him skip and turn aside
> With a hey ho diddle my cat Hyde.
>
> Hey Brown and Fry and Hyde my cats
> That sit on tombstones for your mats.

That is very near folk-rhyme. Probably the prototype is a jingle from the Middle Ages. There are several variants; one is:

> Hey diddle dumpling, my son John
> Went to bed with his trousers on,
> One shoe off and one shoe on,
> Hey diddle dumpling, my son John.

In Smith's version, the jingle is plainly given to a witch. There is a sadistic quality in the games that are devised for the cats; secretive, too: 'when nobody is passing by'. The names are uncatlike, and 'Hyde', at any rate, has connotations for those familiar with a certain story by Robert Louis Stevenson (1850–94).

Most of all, what is fascinating is the way in which Smith pits against the nursery-rhyme directness – short lines, full rhymes – her own deployment of quantity. The last two lines open up the sound – 'my cats/That sit on tombstones' – so that short sharp monosyllables of 'cats', 'that' and 'sit' give place to the unforced resonance of 'tombstones'. 'Tombstones' is itself shut down again with the shorter vowels, 'for', 'your', 'mats'. One does not want to make too much of this, but the quality of the poem is that of an art form, and it is an art form achieved without sacrifice of folk quality. Few verse forms work with such apparent directness. It will require a further chapter to work out the implications of this remark.

9

VERSE FORMS (II)

There are modest and unexpected verse forms that tend to favour feminine qualities. A stanza flourished in the Middle Ages known as the quintain. This is applicable to any stanza of five lines. But the form was taken over by Adelaide Crapsey (1878–1914), termed a cinquain, and issued as a series of separate small poems. Indeed, the cinquain was made so much her own that few have since attempted it. Here is one example, 'November Night':

Listen . . .
With faint dry sound,
Like steps of passing ghosts,
The leaves, frost-crisp'd, break from the trees
And fall.

The metre adheres to a syllable-count. There are two syllables in the first line, four in the second, six in the third, eight in the fourth, two in the last. Yet the relationship between stressed and lightly stressed syllables is essentially iambic, so that the first line is a single foot, the second a dimeter, the third a trimeter, and so on.

The whole gives a sense of gradual expansion until the penultimate line, then a sudden diminution.

Here is another example, 'Amaze':

I know
Not these my hands
And yet I think there was
A woman like me once had hands
Like these.

As with Stevie Smith, the reader tends either to pick up the effect or to miss it totally. In this case, the poem appears to be about time and ageing.

The affinity is clearly with the haiku. This is a Japanese form, consisting of three lines. There is a syllabic count: five syllables, seven syllables, five syllables. Few Anglophone poets have kept to this, even in the many translations there have been from the Japanese, much less in original efforts. One of the exceptions is James Kirkup (b. 1918), a British poet who has lived many years in Japan:

In the village pond
the full moon is shaken by
the first falling leaf.

Usually, however, poets writing in English have considered it sufficient to produce a poem of three lines in free verse, as in this translation, by Geoffrey Bownas and Anthony Thwaite, of a haiku by Nakamura Kusatao (1901–83):

Gentle as my dead friend's hand
Resting on my shoulder,
This autumn sunshine.

In its turn, this freer form of haiku has affinity with the triadic stanza or stepped verse peculiarly associated with William Carlos

Williams. A transitional form may be found in the early work, based on the image and termed 'imagistic', of Ezra Pound (1885–1972). According to Stephen Cushman (*William Carlos Williams and the Meanings of Measure*, New Haven, 1985), Pound originally set out his poem 'In a Station of the Metro' thus:

> The apparition   of these faces   in the crowd
> Petals   on a wet, black   bough.

This hybrid, of haiku and stepped verse, gave rise to the characteristic stanza form used by Williams in his epic poem *Paterson*:

> With evening, love wakens
>   though its shadows
>   which are alive by reason
> of the sun shining –
>   grow sleepy now and drop away
>   from desire
> Love without shadows stirs now
>   beginning to waken
>   as night
> advances . . .

There is a tendency for each line in the triad to be shorter than the preceding one, but no syllable-count is followed. The reader is best advised to treat this as free verse arranged in groups of three lines. The effect is that each line of a triad occupies roughly the same time in being read aloud. Each line of the triad, moreover, is pitched a little lower than the one preceding.

Williams wrote numerous poems after this pattern, especially in his later years: 'To Daphne and Virginia', 'The Orchestra', 'The Pink Locust'. A somewhat earlier poem, collected in 1936, may not be stepped but is in three-line stanzas with approximately the same effect. It has been influential, especially on women poets. The title is incorporated into the poem, and the whole begins:

THE RAPER FROM PASSENACK

was very kind. When she regained
her wits, he said, it's all right, kid,
I took care of you.

What a mess she was in. Then he added,
You'll never forget me now.
And drove her home.

The rest of this poem is a first-person account of the rape told by
the victim, as though in a doctor's surgery. The horrific nature of
the subject-matter is controlled by the deliberate rhythm of the
three-line stanza. Perhaps the best comment is one, by way of
analogy, from Elizabeth Bishop (1911–79) in one of her letters:
'Hopkins's terrible sonnets are terrible – but he kept them short,
and in form.' We shall hear more of sonnets later, but it is through
form that Carlos Williams controls the horrors he portrays.

Reticent poet as she was, Bishop took up this form in her poem
about male aggression, 'Roosters'. The stepping is in a reverse direction to that of Williams, in that the first line of each triad is the
shortest and the final line the longest. This indicates a rising pitch,
each line a little higher than the one preceding. The poem begins:

At four o'clock
in the gun-metal blue dark
we hear the first crow of the first cock . . .

The cock is a kind of image of stupid militarism:

Deep from protruding chests
in green-gold medals dressed,
planned to command and terrorize the rest . . .

As the poem goes on, Bishop shows the terror that lies behind the
aggression, a terror characterized by Peter's denial of the Saviour:

Christ stands amazed,
Peter, two fingers raised
to surprised lips, both as if dazed . . .

But the poem nears its conclusion by stating that there would always be a bronze cock on a pillar to show that even the Prince of the Apostles was forgiven his crime. It is there to convince

All the assembly
that 'Deny deny deny'
is not all the roosters cry.

Unlike Williams, Bishop chooses to rhyme, and indeed to use full rhyme most emphatically.

Sylvia Plath (1932–63), on the other hand, has a poem equally stemming from Williams that rhymes where it touches, so to speak. Nevertheless, though there are divagations from the norm, hers is basically a three-line stanza. This, as is the case with Williams and with Bishop, acts as a container for the anguished account of attempted suicide and contemplated suicide which is her poem 'Lady Lazarus'. It begins:

I have done it again.
One year in every ten
I manage it –

A sort of walking miracle, my skin
Bright as a Nazi lampshade,
My right foot

A paperweight,
My face a featureless, fine
Jew linen.

The poem goes on, employing the stanza to control the painful imagery of the prison-camp, itself a means of disclosing an inner torment. Plath has been much imitated, notably by Anne Sexton (1928–74), Maxine Kumin (b. 1925) and Diane Wakoski (b. 1937). Her imitators, however, seldom have the concern for form that sets a limit even to Plath's more impassioned outcries. Passionate emotion reined in by an apparently arbitrary form is the hallmark of Plath's poetry, even in its earliest phase:

> This was a woman: her loves and stratagems
> Betrayed in mute geometry of broken
> Cogs and disks, inane mechanic whims,
> And idle coils of jargon yet unspoken.

This is a quatrain from a sonnet, 'To Eva', written before Plath was twenty. A sonnet is a short poem with a decidedly set form, to be defined shortly. There are something like twenty sonnets among Plath's juvenilia, including 'Female Author', 'Dirge for a Joker' and 'Sonnet for Satan'. Some inner logic, not immediately apparent, causes this elaborate metrical pattern to figure largely in the production of the shorter poem, in Plath and in many others.

The form in both its centrality and its variety was chronicled by Wordsworth:

> a glow-worm lamp,
> It cheered mild Spenser, called from Faeryland
> To struggle through dark ways; and, when a damp
> Fell round the path of Milton, in his hand
> The thing became a trumpet . . .

The poem from which this has been extracted is itself a sonnet. The form as practised in English has five main characteristics: (1) It has fourteen lines; (2) these fourteen lines are divided into a group of eight (octave) and a group of six (sestet); (3) the sonnet has a volta, or turning-point in thought, usually situated at the end of the octave or the beginning of the sestet; (4) it is written in five-stress lines (though very occasionally six-stress lines have been used); (5) it has a pre-set rhyme scheme, involving an extent of alternation in rhyme. All this is a description, based on the practice of poets; not a prescription of what future poets might do.

The sonnet was invented in Italy in the thirteenth century. It was established as a form by the cycles of sonnets written by Dante and by Petrarch. The latter strongly influenced the sixteenth-century poets Wyatt and Surrey, who have already been noticed with respect to the development of terza rima and of blank verse.

The sonnet as employed by Petrarch was written in eleven-syllable lines (hendecasyllabics) and rhymed a b b a a b b a c d e c d e. Sometimes the sestet appeared as c d c d c d. But in English, the hendecasyllabics turned to five-stressed lines, usually iambic pentameters, and a further rhyme scheme emerged: a b a b c d c d e f e f g g. Writing in the second pattern is much easier. A greater number of different rhymes may be used, and this takes the pressure off a language notoriously short of them.

Milton usually employed the Petrarchan model; thus, in the sonnet on his blindness:

When I consider how my light is spent,	a
Ere half my days in this dark world and wide,	b
And that one talent which is death to hide	b
Lodged with me useless, though my soul more bent	a
To serve therewith my maker, and present	a
My true account, lest he returning chide.	b
'Doth God exact day-labour, light denied?'	b
I fondly ask; but Patience to prevent	a
That murmur, soon replies 'God doth not need	c
Either man's work or his own gifts, who best	d
Bear his mild yoke, they serve him best, his state	e
Is kingly. Thousands at his bidding speed	c
And post o'er land and ocean without rest:	d
They also serve who only stand and wait.	e

The craftsmanship here is masterly. Milton finds four rhymes on '-ent' and four on '-ide', with no contortion of syntax or resort to eccentric vocabulary. How difficult this is to achieve may be discovered by any reader attempting a poem in this exacting form.

Surrey, in introducing the sonnet to England, made it more easy to write by using the second of the two patterns already outlined. That is to say, Surrey employed the English pattern, which requires a maximum of two rhymes per vowel-sound. He also altered the form by ending the fourteen lines with a clinching couplet.

Such was the pattern adopted by Shakespeare. Here is his Sonnet 12:

When I do count the clock that tells the time,	a
And see the brave day sunk in hideous night,	b
When I behold the violet past prime,	a
And sable curls all silvered o'er with white,	b
When lofty trees I see barren of leaves,	c
Which erst from heat did canopy the herd,	d
And summer's green all girded up in sheaves	c
Borne on the bier with white and bristly beard;	d
Then of thy beauty do I question make	e
That thou among the wastes of time must go,	f
Since sweets and beauties do themselves forsake,	e
And die as fast as they see others grow,	f
And nothing 'gainst Time's scythe can make defence	g
Save breed to brave him when he takes thee hence.	g

Notice that both Milton and Shakespeare, different as the patterns of their respective sonnets may seem, preserve the volta, the turning-point. In Milton, it appears after the complaint concerning blindness, with the intervention of the voice of Patience 'to prevent that murmur'. In Shakespeare, the volta appears after the description of time passing, with the questioning 'of thy beauty'.

The distinction made so far, that between the Petrarchan and the English sonnet, is essentially one of metre. A further distinction may be made within the general category, 'sonnet', and it is a rhythmic one. There is a difference that can be heard between the formal sonnet and the sprung sonnet. Shakespeare in the example just quoted is adhering to the iambic norm:

    ˘ ˊ | ˘ ˊ | ˘ ˊ | ˘ ˊ | ˘ ˊ |

When I do count the clock that tells the time . . .

But Shakespeare formal can, in another mood, be Shakespeare sprung. Consider Sonnet 129:

Th'expense of spirit in a waste of shame	a
Is lust in action, and till action lust	b
Is perjured, murd'rous, bloody, full of blame,	a
Savage, extreme, rude, cruel, not to trust,	b
Enjoyed no sooner but despisëd straight,	c
Past reason hunted, and no sooner had,	d
Past reason hated, as a swallowed bait	c
On purpose laid to make the taker mad;	d
Mad in pursuit, and in possession so,	e
Had, having, and in quest to have, extreme,	f
A bliss in proof, and proved, a very woe,	e
Before, a joy proposed, behind a dream.	f
All this the world well knows, yet none knows well	g
To shun the heav'n that leads men to this hell.	g

The first two lines may seem iambic enough. But what about the quatrain as a whole?

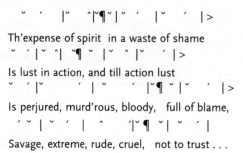

Th'expense of spirit in a waste of shame

Is lust in action, and till action lust

Is perjured, murd'rous, bloody, full of blame,

Savage, extreme, rude, cruel, not to trust . . .

The last line quoted, though unmistakably possessing five stresses, has only two feet, 'extreme' and 'to trust', that can be called rhythmically iambic. Notice that in this particular example, the volta is advanced from the eighth to the thirteenth line. This is a fact not unconnected with the sprung quality of the rhythm. Nearly all of the sonnet tells of the torments of lust. Only with the couplet do we find any turn in the thought, and that is to tell us that the world already knows what has been said, and is powerless to do anything about it.

The sprung sonnet is by no means confined to the looser English form of three quatrains and a couplet. Donne, Shakespeare's near-contemporary, was a master of the sprung sonnet. But he chose to write in the Petrarchan pattern, with only two rhymes in the octave. This was tempered, however, by a sestet clinched, as in Shakespeare, with a final couplet. Even this tempered form is difficult enough to produce. The attraction may be the conflict between turbulent emotion and a tight pattern devised to contain such turbulence. Here is Divine Meditation 7:

At the round earth's imagined corners, blow	a
Your trumpets, angels, and arise, arise	b
From death, you numberless infinities	b
Of souls, and to your scattered bodies go,	a
All whom the flood did, and fire shall o'erthrow,	a
All whom war, dearth, age, agues, tyrannies,	b
Despair, law, chance hath slain, and you whose eyes	b
Shall behold God, and never taste death's woe.	a
But let them sleep, Lord, and me mourn a space,	c
For, if above all these, my sins abound,	d
'Tis late to ask abundance of thy grace	c
When we are there; here, on this lowly ground,	d
Teach me how to repent; for that's as good	e
As if thou hadst sealed my pardon with thy blood.	e

The volta is where it might have been in a more formal sonnet, but it is a volta that theatrically contrasts the sestet with octave. We are brought down from a great trumpeting voice proclaiming the Day of Judgment to a quietly inward meditation on personal sin.

In something of the same sort, the severe Petrarchan form is pulled and racked upon the turbulent patterns of sprung rhythm:

˘　　˘　　　′|　′　|　′|　′˘　|　′˘　˘　|>
All whom war, dearth, age, agues, tyrannies,

˘　′　|　′|　′　|　˘　　′¶|˘　　˘　　˘　′　|>
Despair, law, chance hath slain,　and you whose eyes . . .

This scansion is based upon a rehearsed reading-aloud. It is extraordinary that through all this turbulence one never loses a sense of the five stresses in a line. Yet there are fewer iambic feet even than in Shakespeare's Sonnet 129.

There was a brief hiatus after Wyatt and Surrey got the sonnet settled in England; Wyatt favouring the stricter form, Surrey the English variant. However, when their work was circulated posthumously in an anthology called *Tottel's Miscellany*, not only was the sonnet reborn, but the sonnet sequence emerged. Cycles of sonnets addressed to a putative lover became a kind of norm in Elizabethan poetry. The sonnets of *Astrophel and Stella* by Sir Philip Sidney mostly display Petrarchan octaves. Some have rhymes alternating, rather than in the a b b a pattern. Mostly, each sestet ends in a couplet. Surrey's pattern was followed by Samuel Daniel (1563–1619) in his sequence *To Delia*, and by Michael Drayton (1563–1631) in his sequence *Idea*. Shakespeare, as we have seen, also followed this pattern.

Edmund Spenser (?1552–99) produced in his *Amoretti* a hybrid between the Petrarchan and the English pattern. It has alternating rhymes. There is a linkage not only between the rhymes of the octave, but between those of octave and sestet. The pattern finishes with a couplet on a new rhyme. The pattern runs: a b a b b c b c c d c d e e. But Spenser's example seems to get the worst of both patterns. It is as hard to write as the Petrarchan scheme, and it does not achieve the Petrarchan sense of distinction. The sonnets of Spenser are not his most notable work, and his example has hardly ever been followed.

With the waning of the exuberant Elizabethan and Jacobean age, the sonnet was written only by backward-looking poets. There was a friend of Marvell's, Sir Richard Fanshawe (1608–66); Philip Ayres (1638–1712) – and John Milton. Fanshawe and Ayres are mostly known as translators, and Milton was renowned for his learning.

It is often said that there were no sonnets written between Milton and Wordsworth, and it is true that the form was a rarity in the earlier eighteenth century. However, with the first signs of Romanticism, the sonnet re-emerged, along with an interest in the ballad and in scenery, and with an increasing presence of women practising the art of verse. Poets such as Charlotte Smith (1748–1806), Anna Seward (1747–1809), and Helen Maria Williams (1762–1827) – this last admired by the young Wordsworth – all wrote sonnets. Some were Petrarchan and some not, but almost without exception they adopted the concluding couplet that characterized the English pattern. Typically they dwelt on gloomy scenes, and evoked a mood of melancholy: 'I love thee, mournful sober-suited Night' (Smith); 'Since dark December shrouds the transient day,/And stormy winds are howling in their ire,/Why com'st not Thou?' (Seward); 'Come, gentle Hope! with one gay smile remove/The lasting sadness of an aching heart' (Williams).

Associated with them in style was Thomas Russell (1762–88), who produced too little to have any influence except upon his friend William Lisle Bowles (1762–1850). The *Fourteen Sonnets* of this latter, published in 1789, brought an encomium from the young Coleridge. In a letter to his friend John Thelwall, he wrote: 'Bowles, the most tender and, with the exception of Burns, the only always *always-natural* poet in our language' (17 December 1796). The crucial impact of Bowles, whose specific charm is hard to recover, was on Wordsworth. Probably Bowles was a kind of halfway house in a tradition going back to Milton; a way of learning from Milton without being overcome by the older poet's sometimes Latinate style.

It is certainly true that Wordsworth, when in doubt, expressed himself in the form of the sonnet. While these sonnets often function as *vers de circonstance* – 'On the Death of His Majesty (George the Third)' – some rank among the finest performances in the genre. So far as metrical form is concerned, Wordsworth favoured the Petrarchan pattern. Whatever his variations on this, and there are several, he eschewed (unlike Bowles) the typically English couplet-ending. In that respect, he certainly followed Milton. He never wrote a better sonnet than 'Composed upon Westminster Bridge':

Earth has not anything to show more fair:	a
Dull would he be of soul who could pass by	b
A sight so touching in its majesty:	b
This city now doth like a garment wear	a
The beauty of the morning; silent, bare,	a
Ships, towers, domes, theatres and temples lie	b
Open unto the fields, and to the sky;	b
All bright and glistening in the smokeless air.	a
Never did sun more beautifully steep	c
In his first splendour valley, rock, or hill;	d
Ne'er saw I, never felt, a calm so deep!	c
The river glideth at his own sweet will:	d
Dear God! the very houses seem asleep;	c
And all that mighty heart is lying still!	d

Superb though the sonnet is, one can find signs of the pressure the Petrarchan pattern put upon the author. There is in this, as in other of Wordsworth's sonnets, a degree of archaism. In the best of these sonnets, however, any tendency in this direction is counterbalanced by the unexpectedness, as well as the humanity, of the subject-matter.

Wordsworth, master of the formal sonnet, had his excursions into sprung rhythm as well. His poem on the death of a young daughter has a fine onset:

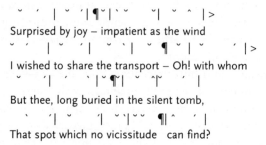

Surprised by joy – impatient as the wind

I wished to share the transport – Oh! with whom

But thee, long buried in the silent tomb,

That spot which no vicissitude   can find?

('Transport' here means a gust of emotion so intense that one is moved from one's normal state of being.) This is Wordsworth at his most Romantic, and practically all the poets usually styled Romantics wrote sonnets.

Shelley wrote only one that is famous, but it is a startling poem – 'Ozymandias' – with a rhyme scheme all of its own – a b a b a c d c e d e f e f – in which 'stone'/'frown' and 'appear'/'despair' should surely count as pararhymes. It has all the appearance of starting off as an English sonnet and rapidly getting out of hand. Yet it is written, or rather it impresses one as being spoken, with such conviction that the subject controls the form.

John Clare (1793–1864), another Romantic poet, wrote an extraordinary series of sonnets on birds: 'The Fern Owl's Nest', 'The Thrush's Nest', 'The Firetail's Nest', and so on. One should not, either, forget the American Romantic, Frederick Goddard Tuckerman (1821–73), who seems to have used the sonnet form as a means of alleviating a constitutional melancholy; or his former tutor at Harvard, Jones Very (1813–80), who wrote upwards of 250 sonnets in a period of religious fervour lasting from autumn 1838 to spring 1840.

Keats, apart from Wordsworth, was the Romantic who most excelled in the sonnet. 'On First Looking into Chapman's Homer';

'When I have fears that I may cease to be'; 'To Sleep'; 'Bright Star! would I were steadfast as thou art' – these have a warmth of personality and a concreteness of utterance that must put them among the most secure masterpieces in the language. The first is Petrarchan in pattern, and the last an English sonnet. But he used all models that came to hand, and in his own sonnet *on* the sonnet produced one entirely of his own.

Although Keats had a bitter reception from the critics of his own time, his reputation has steadily grown since then. His influence can be seen all over the nineteenth century, and nowhere more so than in the work of Gerard Manley Hopkins.

Among Hopkins's poems in this genre are some that are sprung almost beyond recognition. The language is tormented to give 'Felix Randal' and 'Spelt from Sibyl's Leaves' some semblance of the sonnet form. One feels that the poems would have worked anyway, without any such racking into a set pattern.

More in the basic tradition are the so-called 'Terrible Sonnets' of the final period in Hopkins's life, so abruptly ended: 'No worst, there is none'; 'I wake and feel the fell of dark'; 'Thou art indeed just, Lord' and 'To R. B.'. One feels that these, unlike (say) 'Spelt from Sibyl's Leaves', would have been recognized as sonnets by Keats, from whom they ultimately derive. They are probably none the worse for being suited to the pattern they profess.

Unknown in their own time, which was the late 1880s, the sonnets of Hopkins have eclipsed the show sequences of the day: *Sonnets from the Portuguese* by Elizabeth Barrett Browning (1806–61) which the art critic John Ruskin (1819–1900) compared with those of Shakespeare, or *The House of Life* by Dante Gabriel Rossetti (1828–82). The only sequence to compare with the work of Hopkins is *Sonnets of the Wingless Hours* by Eugene Lee-Hamilton (1845–1907), much admired by Ian Fletcher and George MacBeth. These sonnets, however, are currently unread, perhaps because their exquisite versification cannot overcome the depressing nature of their subject, the poet's ill-health.

One would have expected that, with the onset of modernism in the twentieth century, the sonnet would have died a natural death, but it is not so. There are notable examples such as 'Leda and the Swan' (W. B. Yeats), 'Anthem for Doomed Youth' (Wilfred Owen), 'Requiem for the Croppies' (Seamus Heaney), 'The Subway' (Allen Tate), 'Design' (Robert Frost, 1874–1963), 'Piazza Piece' (John Crowe Ransom, 1888–1974), 'The Sunbench' (Mebh McGuckian, b. 1950).

There are even whole sequences such as 'In Time of War' and 'The Quest' by W. H. Auden, 'Glasgow Sonnets' by Edwin Morgan (b. 1920) and 'Funeral Music' by Geoffrey Hill (b. 1932). Robert Lowell (1917–77) and John Berryman (1914–72) expressed themselves in huge quantities of sonnets. Some of those by Lowell, however, were recensions of earlier work in other forms.

Further, Berryman's best efforts, poetically speaking, were in the 'buckled sonnet' form of *The Dream Songs*. The buckled sonnet is a poem which violates many of one's preconceptions concerning the form without altogether taking leave of it. Those of Berryman each consist of three sestets, in a relationship one to another not unlike the propositions found in a logical figure, the syllogism. An example is 'Dream Song 29'. This could be summarized as follows: Henry (the author's other self) felt utter despair; Henry felt measureless regret; nevertheless, Henry never killed anybody. It runs thus:

> There sat down, once, a thing on Henry's heart
> só heavy, if he had a hundred years
> & more, & weeping, sleepless, in all them time
> Henry could not make good.
> Starts again always in Henry's ears
> the little cough somewhere, an odour, a chime.
>
> And there is another thing he has in mind
> like a grave Sienese face a thousand years

would fail to blur the still profiled reproach of. Ghastly,
with open eyes, he attends, blind.
All the bells say: too late. This is not for tears;
thinking.

But never did Henry, as he thought he did,
end anyone and hack her body up
and hide the pieces, where they may be found.
He knows: he went over everyone, & nobody's missing.
Often he reckons in the dawn, them up.
Nobody is ever missing.

Another set of buckled sonnets comprises the 'Twenty-One
Love Poems' of Adrienne Rich (b. 1929). The fourth of these
poems possesses as many as twenty-one lines, but the number of
lines in other items of the sequence ranges more usually between
twelve and sixteen. The implication of sonnet form is to no small
extent owing to the fact that some of the poems relate to and even
answer specific sonnets of Shakespeare.

At this point one could invoke George Meredith (1828–1909),
who wrote a sequence of sixteen-line 'sonnets' called *Modern Love*.
This sequence, however, is perhaps best thought of as a verse novel.
Another poet who wrote a sequence of (mostly) sixteen-line poems,
Caelica, was Fulke Greville (1554–1628). But these have little
feel of being in sonnet form. They are in tone and subject-matter
associated with the religious poems of his near-contemporaries
Donne and George Herbert (1593–1633) which, like those of
Greville, were first published posthumously and in the same year,
1633.

Some modern sonnets, such as a preponderance of those by
Lowell, have no rhyme schemes at all, and so may be the topic of
debate among prosodists. Others make use of pararhyme, and this
is surely one way of lessening the pressure of writing to formal
patterns in a language short of rhymes. Sometimes it may seem

expedient to mix rhyme with pararhyme. The present author has such a work that may serve as an instance: 'Poem for my Daughter'. It is an attempt at evoking the presence of a child who was, in fact, never born:

> I seem to see us going to the zoo,
> You scampering, I pacing. Bears awake
> Your laughter, apes your scorn, turtles your rage –
> 'Great floppy things,' you say, 'what can they do?'
> You run off, and I bellow after you –
> Brown legs flickering under short white frock –
> Standing in impotent call while you glance back
> Laughing, and run off laughing. I run, too,
>
> And bump into a friend, grown middle-aged,
> Point out my curious daughter, paused to see,
> Wave, make you come at last. You shyly wait
> Finger in mouth, huge brown eyes wondering, I
> Resting my hand on your curly dark head;
> Knowing you are not, and may never be.

Elaborate set forms, other than that of the sonnet, have not done too well in English. Many have been attempted: the triolet, the rondeau, the ballade, the pantoum, the limerick, the clerihew. Few of these, however, have been vehicles for any but the lightest of light verse. The two set forms it is proposed to discuss here are the villanelle and the sestina.

The villanelle is really a fifteenth-century French form, usually associated with François Villon (1431–?1463). It had little currency in English until the end of the nineteenth century, when it was (like many other set forms) mostly a vehicle for light verse. The lines of the villanelle may be of any length. The form can be recognized by its rhyme scheme. Of this, the salient factor is that the various stanzas end with alternate refrains, thus: 'And still I say, "To-morrow we shall meet"' and 'In every sound I think I hear her feet'. These refrains will be found to alternate at the end of successive stanzas in the following poem, 'Villanelle' by May Probyn (fl. 1887). The first line of the poem is identical with the second of the refrains:

In every sound, I think I hear her feet
  And still I wend my altered way alone,
And still I say, 'To-morrow we shall meet.'

I watch the shadows in the crowded street –
  Each passing face I follow one by one –
In every sound I think I hear her feet.

And months go by – bleak March and May-day heat –
  Harvest is over – winter well-nigh done –
And still I say, 'To-morrow we shall meet.'

Among the city squares when flowers are sweet,
  With every breath a sound of her seems blown –
In every sound I think I hear her feet.

Belfry and clock the unending hours repeat
  From twelve to twelve – and still she comes in none –
And still I say, 'To-morrow we shall meet.'

O long delayed to-morrow! – hearts that beat
  Measure the length of every minute gone –
In every sound I think I hear her feet.

Ever the suns rise tardily or fleet,
  And light the letters on a churchyard stone, –
And still I say, 'To-morrow we shall meet.'

And still from out her unknown far retreat
  She haunts me with her tender undertone –
In every sound I think I hear her feet,
And still I say, 'To-morrow we shall meet.'

There are twenty-five lines in this poem, and they alternate on only two rhymes. To avoid undue monotony, the writer has to choose his or her subject carefully. Here we have the quality of insistence – an insistent sense of a presence never fully manifested. It is the idea of a lover, either lost or imaginary, never to be encountered by the speaker, who paces the city streets with hope increasingly eroded.

Contemporaries of Probyn such as W. E. Henley (1849–1903), and Henry Austin Dobson (1841–1921) wrote villanelles, but they normally used tetrameters. Here is an example from Oscar Wilde. It is a tribute to Theocritus, the Greek poet who flourished in Sicily round about 280 BC. This villanelle is a tissue of references to the subject-matter of Theocritus' poems, which put forward an idealized notion of the life of shepherds on his native island, home also of Persephone (or Proserpine), who was taken by Pluto, King of the Underworld, to his infernal regions. Wilde's poem suggests that Theocritus, after his own death, languished there with her:

> O Singer of Persephone
>   In the dim meadows desolate,
> Dost thou remember Sicily?
>
> Still through the ivy flits the bee
>   Where Amaryllis lies in state;
> O Singer of Persephone!
>
> Simætha calls on Hecate
>   And hears the wild dogs at the gate;
> Dost thou remember Sicily?
>
> Still by the light and laughing sea
>   Poor Polypheme bemoans his fate;
> O Singer of Persephone!

And still in boyish rivalry
  Young Daphnis challenges his mate;
Dost thou remember Sicily?

Slim Lacon keeps a goat for thee,
  For thee the jocund shepherds wait;
O Singer of Persephone!
Dost thou remember Sicily?

The villanelle has had a strange currency in the twentieth century. It has gone the pentametric way of Probyn rather than the tetrametric one followed by Wilde. Though one cannot say that many villanelles have been written, some of the most distinguished modern poets have left examples of the form, usually in the version which has five stresses to the line. Examples include 'Leap Before You Look', 'If I Could Tell You', 'My Dear One is Mine as Mirrors are Lonely', all by W. H. Auden; 'It is the pain, it is the pain, endures', 'Aubade', 'Missing Dates', 'Reflection from Anita Loos' by William Empson; 'The Waking' by Theodore Roethke; 'Do not go gentle into that good night' by Dylan Thomas (1914–53). Sylvia Plath wrote one, 'Mad Girl's Love Song', that has never been collected: see the *Independent on Sunday*, 9 October 1994.

Another of the set forms that has taken root in English is the sestina. This achieves its form through the repetition of the words found at the end of each line – the words themselves, not just the section of each word that rhymes. The usual pattern is a poem of six six-line stanzas in which the line-endings of the first stanza are repeated in the subsequent five stanzas, each one in a different order, thus: 123456 615243 364125 532614 451362 246531 246. The convention is that the first line of each stanza begins with the last line of the stanza preceding. There is an envoi; that is to say, a truncated concluding stanza. This uses three of the line-endings, by way of summary.

Sir Philip Sidney has a couple of notable examples in his prose romance *Arcadia*. Here is one of them, which the author himself describes as 'austerely maintained sorrowfulness'. The shepherds are mourning the death of their leader, the Duke Basilius:

Since wailing is a bud of causeful sorrow,	1
Since sorrow is the follower of evil fortune,	2
Since no evil fortune equals public damage;	3
Now prince's loss hath made our damage public,	4
Sorrow, pay we to thee the rights of nature,	5
And inward grief seal up with outward wailing.	6

Why should we spare our voice from endless wailing,	6
Who justly make our hearts the seat of sorrow,	1
In such a case where it appears that nature	5
Doth add her force unto the sting of fortune;	2
Choosing, alas, this our theatre public,	4
Where they would leave trophies of cruel damage?	3

Then since such powers conspired unto our damage	3
(Which may be known, but never helped with wailing)	6
Yet let us leave a monument in public	4
Of willing tears, torn hairs, and cries of sorrow,	1
For lost, lost is by blow of cruel fortune	2
Arcadia's gem, the noblest child of nature.	5

O nature doting, old; O blinded nature,	5
How hast thou torn thyself, sought thine own damage	3
In granting such a scope to filthy fortune	2
By thy imp's loss to fill the world with wailing!	6
Cast thy step-mother eyes upon our sorrow:	1
Public thy loss: so, see, thy shame is public.	4

O that we had, to make our woes more public,	4
Seas in our eyes, and brazen tongues by nature,	5

A yelling voice, and hearts composed of sorrow,	1
Breath made of flames, wits knowing naught but damage,	3
Our sports murdering ourselves, our musics wailing,	6
Our studies fixed upon the falls of fortune.	2
No, no, our mischief grows in this vile fortune,	2
That private pains cannot breathe out in public	4
The furious inward griefs with hellish wailing,	6
But forced are to burden feeble nature	5
With secret sense of our eternal damage,	3
And sorrow feed, feeding our souls with sorrow.	1
Since sorrow then concluded all our fortune,	2
With all our deaths show we this damage public:	4
His nature fears to die who lives still wailing.	6

The effect is something like a knell of chimes, and highly suitable for threnody, or mourning-verse.

Earlier in *Arcadia*, Sidney produced a double sestina which is also a threnody: 'Ye goat-herd gods, that love the grassy mountains'. In this case, the line-endings are 'mountains', 'valleys', 'forests', 'music', 'morning', 'evening'. They wind through six stanzas in varying permutations. Then, when they come to stanza 7, they start up over again for a further six stanzas; maintaining, however, the previous pattern. That is to say, stanza 7 has the same line-endings – 'mountains', 'valleys', 'forests', 'music', 'morning', 'evening' – as the first stanza, and in the same order. The ensuing permutations are an exact repeat of the previous order of line-endings, so that stanza 8 corresponds with stanza 2, stanza 9 with stanza 3, and so forth. William Empson said of this double sestina: 'The poem beats, however rich its orchestration, with a wailing and immovable monotony, for ever upon the same doors in vain' (*Seven Types of Ambiguity*, London, 1930; rev. 1947).

Several late nineteenth-century poets, notably A. Mary F. Robinson (1857-1944), attempted the sestina. But it really had its recrudescence in the twentieth century. W. H. Auden, in particular, exploited its peculiar, though limited, qualities. His 'Paysage Moralisé' seems to be a direct imitation of Sidney, with line-endings 'valleys', 'mountains', 'water', 'islands', 'cities', 'sorrow'. There is another example, mysteriously called 'Canzone', in which the line-endings repeat themselves within each stanza, as well as serially through the poem. There are sixty-five lines in 'Canzone', but only five words are employed to end those lines.

The story of this particular form does not end with Auden. John Heath-Stubbs (b. 1918) wrote sestinas earlier in his career ('A Consolation') and later ('The fountain that goes up with plumes of laughter'). John Ashbery (b. 1927) has sestinas on 'The Painter' and on the opera *Faust* by Charles Gounod. Anthony Hecht (b. 1923) has a winter poem, 'Sestina d'Inverno'. There is a sestina by Elizabeth Bishop in tetrameters, whose first line is 'September rain falls on the house'.

Forms like the villanelle and the sestina, however, belong to the category of special effects. Individual poets have produced masterpieces in such set forms as these. However, other than in the sonnet, the genius of English poetry has mostly been shown in continuous metres, such as blank verse and the heroic couplet. One would make a further qualification, though, in respect of stanzaic form.

There is a six-line stanza, rhyming a b a b c c. This has no generally agreed name, but can be called a sexain. It is, perhaps, best considered as a heroic stanza of four lines with an added couplet. Shakespeare used it for his romantic poem *Venus and Adonis*:

> Lo, here the gentle lark, weary of rest,
> From his moist cabinet mounts up on high,
> And wakes the morning, from whose silver breast
> The sun arises in his majesty;
> Who doth the world so gloriously behold
> That cedar-tops and hills seem burnished gold.

On the whole, this has not been as much adopted for narrative poetry as the larger stanzas. Nathaniel Whiting (fl. 1635) used it for his narrative *Albino and Bellama*, and William Bosworth (fl. 1637) for his *Arcadius and Sepha*, but they are exceptions. Wyatt, among several other sixteenth- and seventeenth-century poets, used it for lyric: 'Alas the grief and deadly woeful smart'. It was the vehicle of an elegy for himself by Chidiock Tichborne (?1558–86) – 'My prime of youth is but a frost of cares' – which remains one of the most-frequented Elizabethan poems. The sexain was a key factor in this great age of song, and many poems in this stanza, for example those by Thomas Campion (1567–1620), were set to music.

Docked of a foot in each line, the stanza still proved to be suitable for lyric poetry. William Cartwright (1611–43) has a tetrametric poem, 'To Chloe (who for his sake wished herself younger)':

> There are two births; the one when light
> First strikes the new awakened sense;
> The other when two souls unite,
> And we must count our life from thence:
> When you loved me and I loved you
> Then both of us were born anew.

This is one of many seventeenth-century examples. They look forward to the nineteenth-century lyric, and, by and large, the tetrametric version of sexain has been more utilized for lyric than the pentametric version has for narrative. In the twentieth century, for instance, Theodore Roethke has a fine lyric 'In a Dark Time'. Here, the rhyme scheme is varied to a b b a c c.

There is a seven-line stanza, called rhyme royal. It was adapted from French and Italian models by Chaucer, who used it in his romantic poem of the Trojan Wars, *Troilus and Criseyde*. It is a stanza of seven pentametric lines, rhyming a b a b b c c, and is very versatile. Rhyme royal was the form chosen by Wyatt for his bitter love lyric, 'They flee from me that sometime did me seek'. It was employed by Shakespeare for his narrative on a classical theme, *The Rape of Lucrece*. ('Silly', by the way, at this time meant 'simple' or 'innocent'.)

> Now stole upon the time the dead of night,
> When heavy sleep had closed up mortal eyes;
> No comfortable star did lend his light,
> No noise but owls' and wolves' death-boding cries;
> Now serves the season that they may surprise
> The silly lambs. Pure thoughts are dead and still,
> While lust and murder wake to stain and kill.

Francis Kynaston (1587–1642) in his *Leoline and Sydanis* was one of several who used rhyme royal for narrative poems in the seventeenth century. Phineas Fletcher (1582–1650) turns it to allegory in *The Purple Island*. He extends the last line of each stanza into a hexameter; as does Wordsworth, in the most famous nineteenth-century example of rhyme royal, 'Resolution and Independence':

> My course I stopped as soon as I espied
> The old man in that naked wilderness:
> Close by a pond, upon the further side,
> He stood alone: a minute's space I guess
> I watched him, he continuing motionless:
> To the pool's further margin then I drew;
> He being all the while before me in full view.

In the twentieth century, John Masefield chose rhyme royal for several of his narrative poems, notably *The Widow in the Bye Street* and *Dauber*. It can serve for lyric poems, too, as witness Roethke's exquisite 'I Knew a Woman'. Auden chose it for his 'Letter to Lord Byron', though that poet's best work is in ottava rima.

Ottava rima is an eight-line stanza rhyming a b a b a b c c. It was used in Italy by such narrative poets as Giovanni Boccaccio

(1313–75), Ludovico Ariosto (1474–1533) and Torquato Tasso (1544–95). The influence of these writers on English verse cannot be exaggerated. Chaucer imitated the first of them, Boccaccio, in *Troilus and Criseyde* and elswhere. He introduced ottava rima into English with his 'Monk's Tale' in *The Canterbury Tales*, though his rhyme scheme is a variant: a b a b b c b c. In the sixteenth century, Wyatt used the single stanza in its usual pattern as a basis for individual lyrics, thus:

> Alas, madame! for stealing of a kiss
> Have I so much your mind then offended?
> Have I then done so grievously amiss
> That by no means it may be amended?
> Then revenge you, and the next way is this:
> Another kiss shall have my life ended.
> For to my mouth the first my heart did suck,
> The next shall clean out of my breast it pluck.

In the sixteenth and seventeenth century alike, ottava rima served as the vehicle for large-scale works, such as *Christ's Victory in Heaven* by Giles Fletcher (?1585–1623), brother of the allegorist Phineas, though he, too, varied the basic stanza, and introduced a hexameter for the final line. There were remarkable translations of Italian originals which amount to major poems in English. Outstanding among them is *Orlando Furioso* translated from Ariosto by Sir John Harington (1561–1612); also *Godfrey of Bulloigne*, translated from Tasso's *Gerusalemme liberata* by Edward Fairfax (d. 1635).

The form went on to have a tremendous re-awakening in the early nineteenth century. This was partly a result of a revival of interest in the Italian poets brought about, at least in part, by the scholarly activities of John Herman Merivale (1779–1844). He translated and commented upon the work of Luigi Pulci (1432–84) in *The Monthly Magazine* (1806–7). Byron, who had known Merivale in his youth, made an attempt at translating the same poem, *Morgante maggiore*. This, together with an imitation of Pulci by John Hookham Frere (1769–1846), encouraged Byron to adopt ottava rima for his major satiric poems, *Beppo, The Vision of Judgment* and his masterpiece, *Don Juan*, the English comic epic *par excellence*. Its handling of ottava rima is remarkable for matching the strict stanza form with what appears to be an easy colloquialism. It is done partly by a kind of wild rhyming akin to pararhyme:

> I want a hero: an uncommon want,
>> When every year and month sends forth a new one,
> Till, after cloying the gazettes with cant,
>> The age discovers he is not the true one:
> Of such as these I should not care to vaunt,
>> I'll therefore take our ancient friend Don Juan –
> We all have seen him in the pantomime,
> Sent to the devil somewhat ere his time.

Ottava rima was certainly in the air. Leigh Hunt (1784–1859) translated Ariosto's *Medoro and Cloridano*, and Keats, who was a close friend of his, cast into ottava rima one of his narrative poems, *Isabella; or, The Pot of Basil* – itself, a story to be found in Boccaccio.

The form had a further revival in the twentieth century. Yeats utilized it for some of his finest poems; most notably, 'Sailing to Byzantium' and 'Among Schoolchildren'. Of all the stanzaic forms, ottava rima is probably the one that has given rise to not only the best but the most varied poetry.

The nine-line stanza, too, has had a long run in English. But it is not likely that anyone is writing it now, at least not in the original form given it by Edmund Spenser. The Spenserian stanza, as it has come to be called, is probably based upon ottava rima; rhyming, as that precursor does, a b a b b c b c. There is added an extra line, a hexameter, rhyming with the line immediately previous to it, c.

The effect is majestic and slow-moving. In practice, it takes craftsmanship, after the stanza has come to a full close on the final hexameter, to get the rhythm started again. Spenser shows considerable skill in handling this multi-rhymed pattern in *The Faerie Queene*, through a total of something like 45,000 lines. The final stanza (as usually printed) of this immense undertaking reads:

> Then 'gin I think on that which nature said,
> Of that same time when no more change shall be,
> But steadfast rest of all things, firmly stayed
> Upon the pillars of eternity,
> That is contrare to mutability;
> For all that moveth doth in change delight:
> But thence-forth all shall rest eternally
> With Him that is the God of Sabbath hight:
> O! that great Sabbath God, grant me that Sabbath's sight.

Spenser achieves his control over the stanza by using archaic words, such as 'hight' (for 'named') when it suits him. He also shortens words, using ''gin' for 'begin' and 'contrare' for 'contrary'. Modern verse is thought to be free of conventions, but in fact its attempted relationship with colloquial speech puts such devices as these out of reach.

Though Spenser has been very much imitated, the imitations usually take the form of applying his majestic stanza to romantic or fantastic subjects, where stylization of vocabulary is not out of place. Thus, when the eighteenth century saw a revival of interest in Spenser, James Thomson (1700–48) produced in this stanza form an allegory called *The Castle of Indolence*, portraying an England overcome with sloth. James Beattie (1735–1803), in the same stanza, produced a poem called *The Minstrel*, which told the story of a visionary boy converted by a hoary sage to the path of science.

This may seem a way of defying the metropolitan concerns of the English Augustans. Yet the leader of that school, Pope, began his career with an imitation of Spenser, as did a poet ostensibly his stylistic opposite. That was Keats, who, in his brief maturity, went on to write in the Spenserian stanza one of his finest narrative poems, 'The Eve of St Agnes'. Leigh Hunt, Shelley and the Scottish poets Burns, Scott, Thomas Campbell (1777–1844), all used the form on occasion; Shelley for his elegy on Keats, 'Adonais'. Byron brought it to a further late flowering in the poem that made him famous: his travelogue *Childe Harold's Pilgrimage*.

There is a paucity of examples from the modern era. Still, the Spenserian stanza may lead a partially submerged existence in the nine-lined stanzas of (for example) 'Church Going' by Philip Larkin. The poem goes only a little further in the direction of pararhyme than Spenser, of whom Coleridge remarked that he varied the final vowels as the rhyme required. The final hexameter of Spenser's stanza, however, has in Larkin been subdued to five stresses. Let us remind ourselves of this:

> Once I am sure there's nothing going on
> I step inside, letting the door thud shut.
> Another church: matting, seats, and stone,
> And little books; sprawlings of flowers, cut
> For Sunday, brownish now; some brass and stuff
> Up at the holy end; the small neat organ;
> And a tense, musty, unignorable silence,
> Brewed God knows how long. Hatless, I take off
> My cycle-clips in awkward reverence.

That is as near to the Spenserian stanza as the later twentieth century has gravitated.

There is no point in discussing stanzas larger than the Spenserian. Mostly, they are versions of the ottava rima, with a couplet or so added. It must be remembered, also, that the foregoing description of verse forms does not include all the stanzas of varied line-lengths that have been used for various modes of lyric verse through the centuries. In theory one could apply the term 'canzone' to these, but the word has never become domesticated to English, and the English term 'lyric' would probably do as well. That is, after all, a word which covers Donne's love poems, Keats's 'Odes' and the varied application of stanza form in 'Veteris vestigia flammae' ('Traces of an Ancient Flame') by Thomas Hardy (1840–1928). Because of the variety of verse patterns involved, however, 'lyric' cannot be of much use as a defining term, at least so far as metre is concerned.

A number of the traditional forms now exist in a hybrid way, testimony at once to the rhythmic vigour implicit in their metrical pattern and to the twentieth-century urge towards freer self-expression. For example, before rhyme entered English from medieval France, and well before the time of Chaucer, there were certain forms derived from Anglo-Saxon which allowed considerable dramatic effect without benefit of stanza patterns at all.

Alliterative verse depended upon reiteration of the first consonants of certain words, and this pattern survived well into the period of rhyme. Alliterative metre can be found at its most effective in the work of William Langland (?1330–?1386), the presumed name of whoever it was that wrote the allegorical poem *Piers Plowman*.

Piers Plowman is a poem of some 7,000 lines, each bearing four heavy stresses. Of the words that take those heavy stresses, two in the first half of each line alliterate with each other and with a third stress-word in the second half of the line. The division within each line is marked by a definite pause.

Here, for example, is Piers the Plowman trying to get the people back to work. He is defied by a character called Waster and his friend, an immigrant from Brittany, and sets the allegorically named Hunger upon them:

> Hunger in haste thoo ¶ hent Waster by the maw
> And wrung him so by the womb ¶ that all watered his eyen.

> He buffeted the Bretoner ¶ about the cheeks
> That he looked like a lantern ¶ all his life after.
> He beat them so both ¶ he burst near their maws
> Nor had Piers with a pease-loaf ¶ prayed Hunger him bileve
> They had been dead and dolven, ¶ nor deem thou none other.

('Thoo' = 'then'; 'hent' = 'took'; 'womb' = 'stomach'; 'eyen' = 'eyes'; 'maws' = 'stomachs'; 'dolven' = 'buried'.)

This is a description of people suffering from hunger because they will not work. The alliterative pattern is highly suited to its task of conveying strife and physical stress.

There are many parallels that could be cited. Quite independently of *Piers Plowman*, somebody totally unknown (fl. ?1375) wrote a poem based on Arthurian legend – legends of the Round Table – called *Sir Gawain and the Green Knight*. Here is part of a description of Sir Gawain struggling through a winter landscape – presumably that of Cheshire or south Lancashire, whence emanates the dialect of the poem:

> Now nighs the New Year ¶ and the night passes,
> The day drives to the dark ¶ as Drighten bids;
> But wild weathers of the world ¶ wakened thereout,
> Clouds cast keenly ¶ the cold to the earth,
> With nigh enough of the North ¶ the naked to tene;
> The snow snittered full snart ¶ that snaped the wild;
> The werbland wind ¶ wapped from the high,
> And drove each dale full ¶ of drifts full great.

('Drighten' = 'God'; 'tene' = 'torment'; 'snittered' = 'sleeted'; 'snaped' = 'nipped'; 'wild' = 'wild creatures'; 'werbland' = 'whistling'; 'wapped' = 'gusted'.)

There are usually three rather than two alliterated stress words in the first half of each line. The poem, unlike *Piers Plowman*, is sectionalized, and at the end of each section is a bob or short stanza of four lines that rhyme a b a b. So the author of *Sir Gawain and the Green Knight* gets the best of both worlds, rhyme as well as alliteration.

Francis Berry wrote a celebrated essay on *Sir Gawain*. More than that, he applied much of what he learned in studying this poem and its alliterative counterparts to his own work. He is especially strong in expressing scenes of effort and danger. Here, in an early poem called *The Iron Christ*, a giant statue is being dragged up a mountain by a steam train:

> The driver turns his face, his arm to throttle
> Levering steam, but, with a cursing, spin
> The driving-wheels, skidding upon raw rails,
> Circuiting vainly, then grab, heel over rods,
> Pistons pant, valves hiss, wheels grip, groan, grab.

The alliteration is not so precisely patterned as in the medieval poems, because it is only one of several devices to hold the verse together. There is also an element of assonance, that is to say vowel-agreement, as in 'turns' and 'cursing', 'spin' and 'skidding'. But, though distinctively modern, the verse has learned from the medieval exemplars. Partly, it is a matter not only of congruence in style but also of congruence in action. Francis Berry is writing of earthy physical encounters. Here is a building – a cathedral – disintegrating, in his poem *Fall of a Tower*:

> Struts straddle; West Front
> Walks apart, begins ungainly waddle,
> Collapses on its face; brick and mortar
> Flee yelling from their stocks; huge blocks
> Jerk bounding parabolas, booming
> Tomb-slabs throw sepulchral cart-wheels;
> Roof rives asunder, and in gasps
> Buttresses fall flat.

As well as alliteration and assonance, here use is made of rhyme. This admixture of binding agents is favoured by certain modern poets. One could mention Peter Redgrove, Seamus Heaney, Ted Hughes (at least in his earlier work), Stevie Smith, Galway Kinnell (b. 1927), all of whom have an ear for the medieval without sacrificing their sense of the modern. It is no coincidence that each one has more than a touch of the shaman, or spirit-healer.

This is, of course, a further way by which free verse works. As well as the interplay between the lines of thrust and reception, already detailed in Chapter 7, there is an alliterative pattern and, usually, an interplay of assonance as well. Free verse is not so free as it has been represented.

One might be tempted at this point to argue the same for other verse forms. Concrete poetry, first named by Eugen Gomringer (b. 1924), was popular during the 1960s and 1970s. It consists of the poem taking visual form on the page and simulating (say) a flotilla of small boats, or mixing the letters on the page with graphics and photographs, or engaging in a form of pun, as with a one-line poem by Edwin Morgan, 'Siesta of a Hungarian Snake':

s sz sz SZ sz SZ sz Zs zs ZS zs zs z

Such an art is essentially a mixed genre, not defined by its rhythm. It belongs either to one of the branches of drawing, or possibly to some kind of performance art, as does sound poetry.

Sound poetry was another branch activity that flourished in the 1960s. Mostly it was composition through noises rather than articulated words. The effect depended on the person producing the noises. Anyone who saw, for example, Ernst Jandl (fl. 1960s and 1970s) in performance is unlikely to forget the experience. A wonderful range of bickering and brattle, accompanied by grimaces, would be employed to project such a poem as 'Schützengraben' (i.e. 'Trench'). It begins:

schtzngrmm
schtzngrmm
t-t-t-t

```
t-t-t-t
grrrmmmmm
t-t-t-t
s-----c------h . . .
```

These are battle noises. But the poem on the page gives only a faint idea of what is projected in the theatre. Essentially, this is performance art, outside the criteria normally adduced for literature.

Sound poetry is less heard of in the 1990s. This may be because it has been overtaken by events. There is a great deal of what purports to be poetry on the concert platform or the stage rather than in the book.

This is not an attack upon the recital. There is not an analysis in this book that does not depend on a text being read aloud. Poetry is at its best when being spoken. It needs, at the very least, to be heard in the head. Many people cannot get on with a text in verse because they read it at the speed they read their morning newspaper, and fail to hear the rhythm. Reading aloud is a calculated, even a critical, exercise. The reader is trying to extract the meaning from the text, and in this context meaning includes rhythm.

There is, however, a distinction to be made. A good deal of recent verse works the other way round from the poetry that has been described in this and earlier chapters. On the page such recent verse may seem conventional, with what look like stereotyped rhythms and conventional rhymes. But such verse can certainly wake up when subjected to the performance techniques (say) of Benjamin Zephaniah (b. 1958) or Milton Smalling (fl. 1980s). What the 'poem' transpires as, in cases such as theirs, is a score for performance. The meaning is being pushed into the text by the performer, not being drawn out of it by the reader.

For better or worse, that seems to be the way poetry is going as we draw near to the end of the century. Popular music began acquiring a conceptual content at the same time as poetry came to be chanted at what can only be called 'occasions'. Inevitably, the gap between popular music and chanted poetry diminished. Rhythm, therefore, increasingly depended on a particular performer. It cannot nowadays always be discussed as an entity integral to a text. In this respect, it differs from almost all poetry of the past.

The works from the past that survive do so because of their ability to speak beyond their period. We have the sensation of hearing the voices of their authors. There are always going to be alterations of taste which subjugate one writer and bring another into prominence. But there is usually something to disagree about; something which can be pointed out as a text, with definable properties.

The case is quite different with popular music. There, the interpretation takes over from the text. The text is recreated each time a new performer chooses to realize it. It is possible for an entertainer such as Frank Sinatra to impart to a trivial love song a great measure of intensity. This does not make the love song any the less trivial. The intensity is in the performance.

At this time of writing, the technique that patterned the work of those whom we regard as great poets seems to be in the process of becoming mislaid or forgotten. We are being cut off from our cultural past. Instead of the book, the tangible form of the popular entertainer demands our attention. He or she does the interpreting for us. There are those, of course, who would feel that to be an advantage. We can only hope that the era of mixed genre which is now upon us will continue to produce collaborative arts entertaining at the moment. Whether or not they manage to survive into a future is another question.

Glossary

alliteration   repetition of consonants, especially at the beginning of related words.

alliterative metre, alliterative verse   a form of verse, chiefly used in medieval times, in which the shape of the line is determined not by rhyme but by the repetition of consonants within the line on key words, e.g. 'In a summer season when soft was the sun'.

amphibrach   metrical foot featuring a lightly stressed syllable, a heavily stressed syllable, and a lightly stressed syllable, in that order, e.g. 'redouble'.

anapaest   metrical foot featuring two lightly stressed syllables followed by a heavily stressed syllable, e.g. 'repossess'.

assonance   repetition of vowels, especially in the case of related or emphatic words.

ballad metre   four-line stanzas, with four stresses in the first and third lines and three stresses in the second and fourth lines.

blank verse   unrhymed five-stress lines: dramatic and flexible in character (Shakespearian), or heavily stressed and (generally) slow-moving (Miltonic), or predominantly medium to light in stress (Wordsworthian).

bob   a short line at the end of a stanza, giving the effect of having been curtailed.

cadenced verse   a form of free verse, often in long lines, based on the highly wrought prose of the Bible (Authorised Version), especially associated with Walt Whitman and the 'Beast, Bird and Flower' poems of D. H. Lawrence.

caesura   a slight pause occurring mid-line, not necessarily requiring especial marking of its occurrence, e.g. 'And never lifted up a single stone', where the caesura occurs after the word 'up'. When there is a pause heavy enough to variegate the rhythm, it may be signified with a mark, thus: ¶

cavalier lyric   song-lyric, at its zenith during the events leading up to the English Civil War in the seventeenth century, tending to gallantry; using a four- or six-lined stanza rhyming alternately, and associated particularly with Jonson, Herrick and Lovelace.

cinquain   a poem of five lines, especially associated with Adelaide Crapsey: usually with two syllables in the first line, four in the second, six in the third, eight in the fourth and two in the last.

concrete poetry   a form whose significance is partly, and sometimes predominantly, a result of its visual shape on the page; thus 'Easter Wings', by George Herbert, is shaped like a pair of wings.

couplet   two lines of verse linked together, usually by a rhyme.

dactyl   metrical foot consisting of one stressed syllable followed by two stressed syllables, e.g. 'pulverize'.

dimeter   a line consisting of two main stresses, e.g. 'The scented hours'.

end-stopping   an end-stopped line is one where the sense and rhythm undergo a partial cessation or heavy pause at the end of the line.

enjambment   the name given to an effect whereby sense and rhythm run over the line-ending and on into the next line; the opposite of 'end-stopping'. It can be signified by the mark >.

feminine ending   the end of a line whose final syllable is lightly stressed, or one whose two final syllables are (in sequence) heavily stressed and lightly stressed, e.g. 'a wave interminably flowing', where 'flowing' is the feminine ending.

foot   the metrical basis of a line; that is to say, a metrical pattern identified by the disposition of heavy and light stresses (see, for example, 'iamb' and 'amphibrach'). Its conclusion may be signified by the mark |.

free verse   a form of verse whose distinction is not to conform to a pre-set pattern. It can take the shape of a more varied mode of blank verse, as in T. S. Eliot; of cadenced verse, related to Biblical prose, as in Walt Whitman; or, as free verse proper, a verse formed by a line that thrusts against a line that receives that thrust, or any related pattern of thrust and reception of thrust, as in Wallace Stevens and William Carlos Williams. Thrust may be signified by the mark » and reception of thrust may be signified by the mark «.

haiku   a form adapted from Japanese poetry where it is defined as a three-line poem, the first line of which has five syllables, the second line of which has seven syllables, and the third line of which has five syllables. Often in English, however, the term is applied to any poem of an imagistic tendency so long as it consists of no more than three lines.

hendecasyllabics a line consisting of eleven syllables, usually with a feminine ending.

heroic couplet five-stress lines rhyming in pairs.

hexameter a line consisting of six stresses; often (though not necessarily) imitative of the Greek or Latin catalectic line, which usually consists of six feet: five dactyls and a spondee (or curtailed dactyl).

iamb the most frequently used metrical foot in English, consisting of one lightly stressed syllable followed by one heavily stressed syllable, e.g. 'revolve'.

internal rhyme a rhyme occurring in mid-line, either in addition to rhymes occurring where they normally occur, at the end of lines, or as a special effect picking up a sound from elsewhere in a piece of verse on the whole unrhymed.

inversion an inverted foot is one that reverses one's normal expectation, e.g. a trochee occurring at the beginning of a line otherwise iambic: 'Wisdom and spirit of the universe!'.

masculine ending the end of a line whose final syllable is heavily stressed.

metre the ground-plan or blueprint of a piece of verse, indicative of a pattern where heavily stressed syllables are interspersed with more lightly stressed syllables.

octave a piece of verse eight lines long with alternating (or otherwise patterned) rhymes; a term usually employed to describe the earlier (and larger) section of a sonnet.

ottava rima an eight-line stanza whose first six lines rhyme alternately but which ends in a couplet; perhaps the most versatile stanza form in English.

outride a term invented by Hopkins to define a kind of syllable so lightly stressed as not to require metrical indication. In such a line as 'How to keep – is there any any, is there none such', the first 'is there', and its repetition five syllables further on, are outrides.

pararhyme rhyme deliberately imperfect, to create a kind of echo effect. There are several sub-varieties: 'wire'/'war' is three-quarter rhyme; 'on'/ 'stone' is half-rhyme; 'on'/'organ' is quarter-rhyme; 'best'/'stuffed' is eighth-rhyme.

pentameter a line consisting of five main stresses.

performance poetry a mode, popular in the 1980s and 1990s, in which the literary content is comparatively slight and often conventional, and the main effect is produced by the way in which the poetry is spoken or, indeed, acted out on stage.

poetic diction an ostentatiously literary style, involving archaisms and nonce-words, usually employed by inferior poets to solve what are for them difficult problems in the reconciliation of meaning with rhyme, e.g. 'Is she nested? Does she kneel/In the twilight stilly?'. Here, 'stilly' is diction for 'still', in order to manufacture a rhyme for 'lily'.

quantity vowels can be of different lengths: for example, the 'o' varies in the three words, 'loss', 'rose', 'woe'. The relative length of vowels, termed 'quantity', was the prime rhythmic constituent of Greek and Latin poetry, and it can be used as an element in English. In English, however, it is always subordinate to stress. But skilful poets can play it off against stress as a species of counterpoint in the form of verse known as syllabics.

quatrain a stanza of four lines.

quintain a name for a stanza of five lines, usually rhymed, to distinguish it from the often unrhymed cinquain.

rhyme the exact echoing of a sound at the end of one line by the sound at the end of another line.

rhyme royal a stanza composed of seven five-stress lines rhyming a b a b b c c.

rhythm the working machine of poetry, as metre is its ground-plan or blueprint. It is the variegation of metre according to the tones of the voice in which a poem is read aloud; this, in its turn, being governed by both meaning and stress pattern.

sestet the second part of a sonnet, consisting of six lines, as distinct from the larger first part, the octave. The first four rhymes alternate, and are often (though not necessarily) followed by a couplet.

sestina a form of verse that uses the repetition of words at the end of lines instead of a repeated rhyme scheme. A frequent pattern is a poem of six six-line stanzas in which the line-endings of the first stanza are repeated in the subsequent five stanzas, each one in a different order, e.g. 123456, 615243, 346125, 532614, 451362, 246531.

sextain a six-line stanza, usually composed of a heroic stanza of four lines rhyming alternately with an added couplet: a b a b c c.

Skeltonics very short lines, usually dimeters, rhyming, but with no set metrical pattern; named after the sixteenth-century poet John Skelton who used them a great deal, if he did not actually invent them.

sonnet a fourteen-line poem, consisting of two parts: one of eight lines, called an octave, one of six lines, called a sestet. The octave either rhymes a b b a a b b a (Petrarchan) or a b a b c d c d (English). The sestet either rhymes c d e c d e (though there are variants of this) or e f e f g g – and that concluding couplet, g g, favoured by the 'English' model, makes a good deal of difference. Octave and sestet are separated not only by metrical form but an alteration in the line of argument, termed a volta. The twentieth century has seen developments of the sonnet proper; in particular, the buckled sonnet, which alludes to the sonnet form rather than following it exactly, e.g. *The Dream Songs* by John Berryman and 'Twenty-One Love Poems' by Adrienne Rich.

sound poetry composition through noises rather than articulated words, whose effect largely depends on the person producing the noises.

spondee metrical foot consisting of two successive stressed syllables, e.g., at the end of a line, 'no more'.

sprung verse, sprung rhythm a term invented by Hopkins to describe what is in fact the norm in much English verse, whereby the pattern of heavy stress is the determining factor while the number of light syllables in proportion to those that are stressed is a variable. Hopkins himself declared that each metrical foot had one principal stress and that the other syllables in the foot were more or less lightly stressed.

stanza a metrical and rhyming pattern of between three and ten lines (sometimes more), repeated several times over to form the structure of a poem. The following are the main varieties.

– **ballad stanza** two lines of four stresses alternating with two lines of three stresses, rhyming alternately; similar to many varieties of the hymn stanza, but freer in rhythm and more excited in style. Later and more literary versions have many variants.

– **Burns stanza** three four-stress lines rhyming a a a; then a two-stress line, often with a feminine ending, featuring a b-rhyme; then a further four-stress line rhyming with the previous four-stress lines; then a concluding two-stress line, rhyming with the previous two-stress line. Similar to the Habbie stanza, but more varied rhythmically.

– **elegiac stanza** composed of four five-stress lines, rhyming alternately; similar to the heroic stanza, but less varied in rhythm and quieter in tone.

– **Habbie stanza** see Burns stanza.

– **heroic stanza** composed of four five-stress lines, rhyming alternately; similar to the elegiac stanza, but more varied in rhythm and more public in tone.

– **Horatian stanza** named after the Latin poet Horace, who used it for his odes, this consists of four lines, two longer followed by two shorter. It may be rhymed as in Marvell or unrhymed as in Collins.

– **hymn stanza** two lines of four stresses alternating with two lines of three stresses, rhyming alternately; similar to the ballad stanza, but more formal in rhythm and, on the whole, quieter in tone. There are many variants, such as four lines each of four stresses rhyming alternately; or six lines consisting of four stresses followed by a couplet of four-stress lines.

– **In Memoriam stanza** a stanza of four four-stress lines rhyming a b b a, invented by Jonson and most famously used by Tennyson in his elegy, 'In Memoriam'.

– **Spenserian stanza** a stanza of nine five-stress lines based on the ottava rima, and rhyming for its first eight lines, as that does, a b a b b c b c; but there is added a ninth line, also rhyming on c, which has six stresses.

– **triadic stanza** see stepped verse.

stepped verse verse written in the triadic (or three-line) stanza. Often, as with William Carlos Williams, each line in the triad is shorter than the one preceding, but Elizabeth Bishop has a variant in which the first line of each triad is the shortest and the last line the longest, while in Sylvia Plath, as might be expected, there is no norm. Stepped verse may be rhymed, in which case all three lines usually take the same rhyme, or are unrhymed.

stress the amount of weight given to a given syllable. The four most readily ascertainable varieties are the ones following.

– **primary** heavy or strong stress, which may be signified by the mark ´.

– **secondary** medium stress, which may be signified by the mark ˆ.

   – **tertiary** medium-light stress, which may be signified by the mark ˋ.

   – **weak** light stress, which may be signified by the mark ˇ.

It must be remembered that stresses are, to some extent, relative, affected by their position in a line and by the other stresses surrounding them. An example of a line using all four weights of stress is Marvell's

    ˆ   ˇ   ˇ   ˊ   ˇ   ˋ   ˇ   ˊ

   Had we but world enough and time.

syllabics a form of verse whereby the syllable count of the several lines is the measure of form, thus: 'Dürer would have seen a reason for living'. This is the first line of a poem by Marianne Moore in six-line stanzas featuring a syllable count in the lines, respectively, of 11, 10, 14, 8, 8, 3. It is not, however, possible to get rid of stress as the prime constituent of English verse, so the effect is to counterpoint the syllabic count against the stress pattern. Characteristically, in order to prevent the stress pattern from swamping the syllabic count, poems written in syllabics tend to a predominance of medium and light stresses, and also to an extent of enjambment.

tercet a three-line verse form, usually applied to each individual section of a sequence that comprises terza rima.

terza rima three-line sections, interlinking one with another. The first and third lines of each section rhyme, and the second line of that section rhymes with the first and third lines of the next section, thus: a b a b c b c d c d e d e f e. Any series of three-line sections, also known as tercets, may brought to a conclusion by a single line rhyming with the second line of the three-line section immediately preceding. Dante, who invented the form, wrote his sections in hendecasyllablcs, but in English they tend to be five-stress lines, sometimes with rhymes alternating between masculine and feminine endings.

tetrameter a line consisting of four main stresses.

trimeter a line consisting of three main stresses.

trochee metrical foot consisting of one heavily stressed syllable followed by one lightly stressed syllable, e.g. 'forward'.

villanelle a form related to terza rima, in which the rhymes alternate throughout a sequence of tercets, thus: a b a   a b a   a b a   a b a. A salient feature is that each tercet ends in a refrain, and that there are only two refrains alternating throughout the poem. The set of tercets is rounded off with a quatrain in which the two refrains at last come together, one capping the other. An additional refinement is that the first line of the poem is identical with the refrain at the end of the second tercet. This has a unique effect of rounding-off, when the two refrains immediately follow one another at the end of the poem. There are numerous variants, and the villanelle can as readily be in four-stress lines as in five-stress lines, but alternate rhyming and the alternating refrains are a key characteristic of the form.

volta a turn of thought that comes between the octave of a sonnet and its sestet, so that the metrical form of the poem is reinforced by an alteration in its line of argument.

SELECTED BIBLIOGRAPHY

This is a selection from the books and articles consulted. Care has been taken to make sure that the selection represents a range of opinon concerning metre and rhythm.

Agenda. 10 (1972/3); Special issue on rhythm; contributions by
    W. H. Auden, Anne Beresford, Keith Bosley, Basil Bunting, *et al.*

Attridge, Derek. *The Rhythms of English Poetry*, London: Longman (1982).

Barry, Sister M. M. *An Analysis of the Prosodic Structure of Selected Poems
    of T. S. Eliot*, Washington, DC: Catholic University of America Press
    (1969).

Baum, P. F. *The Principles of English Versification*, Cambridge, Mass.:
    Harvard University Press (1922).

Berry, Francis. *Poetry and the Physical Voice*, London: Routledge (1962).

Blackstone, Bernard. *Practical English Prosody*, London: Longman Green
    (1965).

Bly, Robert. 'Whitman's Line as a Public Form', *The American Poetry
    Review* 15 (1986).

Botting, Kevin. *English to GCSE*, Unit 8 'Introduction to Verse: A
    Discussion of Rhythm', Southampton: Ashford Press Publishing
    (1987).

Cable, Thomas. *The English Alliterative Tradition*, Philadelphia: University
    of Pennsylvania Press (1991).

Chatman, Seymour. *A Theory of Meter*, The Hague: Mouton (1965).

Couper-Kuhlen, Elizabeth. *An Introduction to English Prosody*, London:
    Edward Arnold (1986).

Crapsey, Adelaide. *A Study in English Metrics*, New York: Knopf (1918).

Crombie, Winifred. *Free Verse and Prose Style*, London: Croom Helm (1987).

Crystal, David. *The English Tone of Voice*, London: Edward Arnold (1975).

Cureton, Richard D. *Rhythmic Phrasing in English Verse*, London and New York: Longman (1992).

Cushman, Stephen. *William Carlos Williams and the Meanings of Measure*, New Haven: Yale University Press (1985).

Dobrée, Bonamy. *Histriophone: A Dialogue on Dramatic Diction* (Hogarth Essays no. 5) London: Hogarth Press (1925).

Docherty, Thomas. *John Donne, Undone*, London: Methuen (1986).

Fussell, Paul. *Poetic Meter and Poetic Form*, rev. edn, New York: Random House (1979).

Fraser, G. S. *Metre, Rhyme and Free Verse*, London: Methuen (1970).

Geiger, Don. *The Sound, Sense, and Performance of Poetry*, Chicago: Scott, Foresman (1963).

Gross, Harvey. *Sound and Form in Modern Poetry*, Ann Arbor: University of Michigan Press (1964).

Hamer, Enid. *The Metres of English Poetry*, London: Methuen (1969).

Harding, D. W. *Words into Rhythm*, Cambridge: Cambridge University Press (1976).

Hardison, O. B., Jr. *Prosody and Purpose in the English Renaissance*, Baltimore: Johns Hopkins University Press (1989).

Hartman, C. O. *Free Verse*, Princeton: Princeton University Press (1980).

Hollander, John. *Rhyme's Reason: A Guide to English Verse*, New Haven and London: Yale University Press (1981; enlarged edn 1989).

—— *Vision and Resonance*, 2nd edn, New Haven: Yale University Press (1985).

Holloway, Sister Marcella Marie. *The Prosodic Theory of Gerard Manley Hopkins*, Washington, DC: Catholic University Press (1947).

Hopkins, Gerard Manley. *Journals and Papers*, ed. Humphry House and Graham Storey, Clarendon Press: Oxford (1959).

Kemp, Harry 'An Age of Vers Libre', repr. in *Poems for Mnemosyne: Selected Poems*, Crediton, Devon: privately published (1993).

—— *An Essay and Poems*, Crediton, Devon: privately published (1993).

Kenyon Review, The. 18 (1956); contributions by Seymour Chatman, John Crowe Ransom, Arnold Stein, Harold Whitehall, *et al.*

Leech, Geoffrey N. *A Linguistic Guide to English Poetry*, London: Longman (1969).

Levin, Samuel R. *Linguistic Structures in Poetry*, The Hague: Mouton (1962).

McAuley, James. *Versification: A Short Introduction*, Detroit: Michigan State University Press (1966).

Ohio Review, The. 38 (1987); contributions by Robert Bly, Wayne Dodd, Edward Hirsch, William Mathews, Roger Mitchell, Mary Oliver, Bin Ramke, *et al.*

Opie, Iona and Peter. *The Lore and Language of Schoolchildren*, Oxford: Clarendon Press (1959).

Patmore, Coventry. *Essay on English Metrical Law*, ed. Sister Mary Augustina Roth, Washington, DC: Catholic University Press (1961).

Piper, W. B. *The Heroic Couplet*, Cleveland: Case Western Reserve University Press (1969).

Preminger, Alex, and T. V. F. Brogan (eds), *The New Princeton*

Encyclopedia of Poetry and Poetics, Princeton: Princeton University Press (1993).

Pyle, Fitzroy. 'Pyrrhic and Spondee: Speech Stress and Metrical Accent in English Five-Foot Iambic Verse Structure', *Hermathena* 107 (1968–9), 49–74.

——— 'The Rhythms of the English Heroic Line: An Essay in Empirical Analysis', *Hermathena* 53 (1939), 100–26.

Robinson, Ian. *Chaucer's Prosody: A Study of the Middle English Verse Tradition*, Cambridge: Cambridge University Press (1971).

Roethke, Theodore. *On the Poet and his Craft*, ed. Ralph J. Mills, Jr, Seattle: University of Washington Press (1965).

Saintsbury, George. *Historical Manual of English Prosody*, London: Macmillan (1926).

Steele, Timothy. *Missing Measures: Modern Poetry and the Revolt against Meter*, Fayetteville: University of Arkansas Press (1990).

Tendril Magazine 18 (1984); contributions by Denise Levertov, Stanley Plumly, *et al.*

Trager, G. L. and H. L. Smith, Jr. *An Outline of English Structure* (Studies in Linguistics Occasional Papers no. 9) Norman: Battenburg Press (1951).

Wesling, Donald. *The New Poetries: Poetic Form since Coleridge and Wordsworth*, Lewisburg: Bucknell University Press (1985).

Weygand, Norman, S. J. (ed.) *Immortal Diamond: Studies in Gerard Manley Hopkins*, New York: Sheed and Ward (1949); contributions by John Louis Bonn, S. J., Walter J. Ong, S. J., *et al.*